BIBLE BOOSTER SHOTS FOR THE BELIEVER

I0161847

ENDORSEMENT
by
Lynn Williams

As a believer in Christ Jesus, you come to realize how important it is to feed your spiritual body in order to maintain a healthy life in Christ. In this book, Arnie Derksen has captured the very essence of what it takes to remain strong and healthy while living under the Word of God. Arnie provides the reader with some simple step-by-step instructions to guide you through every area of life to become victoriously strong and prosperous, both in wealth and in health.

These spiritual booster shots are just what believers need to protect their spiritual immune systems from the attacks of the enemy, Satan; the world; and their own sinful flesh. I found *Bible Booster Shots for the Believer* to be a very helpful tool. You can carry this book with you and refer to its lists as your personally prescribed doses of God's Word when you find yourself in need of a boost from God to get you through whatever trials or circumstances you are facing at that moment; and later, you can sit down and read the referenced Scriptures in their entirety for yourself so you can see how the Word has successfully protected you through attacks. These spiritual booster shots are simply quick and simple reminders of how we are to live each day as authentic Christians, and getting a shot in our spiritual arm from God's Word will be just what each of us needs to remain genuine as we learn to spread the gospel and not the spiritual viruses of the lust of the eye, the lust of the flesh, and the pride of life.

So if you want to protect yourself from those unseen "principalities . . . powers . . . rulers of the darkness of this age . . . [and] spiritual hosts of wickedness in heavenly places" *(Ephesians 6:10–18)* that are sent by Satan to attack the weak parts of your spiritual immune system, then I suggest you take a shot at reading and referring to this book as you prevent any further attacks from being successful in your walk with God. Keep your booster shots up to date by reading God's Word daily so you will be found immune to the attacks that will kill, steal, and destroy you if you don't.

May God Bless You With a Huge Dose of His Word!

"But the Lord is faithful, who will establish you
and guard you from the evil one."
—2 Thessalonians 3:3

The Royal Candlelight Presents

BIBLE BOOSTER SHOTS FOR THE BELIEVER:

Boost Your Spiritual Immune System Against Evil Viruses

by Arnie Derksen

Royal Candlelight Christian Publishing Company

"Royalty in the Making"

The Royal Candlelight: Bible Booster Shots for the Believer
© 2013 by Arnie Derksen

Royal Candlelight Christian Publishing Company
"Royalty in the Making"

Royal Candlelight Christian Publishing
P.O. Box 3021
Fontana, California 92334
www.royalcandlelight.com
info@royalcandlelight.com
Internet TV website: Ustreamtv.com (Royal Candlelight)

Editor: Rachel Starr Thomson
Graphic & Media Arts Designer: Talon Williams
Book Layout Designer: Nicole Dunlap
Sales & Marketing Director: Paul Williams
Website Designer: Ebenezer Jesutimi

Unless otherwise indicated, all Scripture quotations are taken from the *New King James Version.* Copyright © 1979, 1980, 1982 by Thomas Nelson, Inc. Used by permission. All rights reserved.

Scripture quotations marked NASB are from the *New American Standard Bible©* 1960, 1962, 1963, 1968, 1971, 1972, 1973, 1975, 1977, by The Lockman Foundation. Used by permission.

ALL RIGHTS RESERVED
No portion of this publication may be reproduced, stored in a retrieval system, or transmitted in any form or by any means—electronic, mechanical, photocopy, recording or any other except for brief quotations in printed reviews or articles, without the prior permission of the publisher.

ISBN-10: 978-0615832944
ISBN-13: 0615832946

Printed in the United States of America

ACKNOWLEDGEMENTS

To my wife, "Indy"

With gratitude and love to my wife, Nancy E. Derksen,

for her continued support and prayers in my life.

To my pastor

Thanks to Dr. Joshua Beckley

for encouraging me to publish this book.

To Lynn Williams

A BIG THANK YOU for her enthusiasm for this project.

Lynn's careful and meticulous copying of the manuscript

also deserves a great big thank-you.

Table of Contents

BIBLE BOOSTER SHOTS FOR THE BELIEVER

Boost Your Spiritual Immune System Against Evil Viruses

SPIRITUAL PRESCRIPTION'S FOR THE BELIEVER

FOREWORD

by
Dr. Joshua Beckley, PhD

In this book, Arnie Derksen has taken the time to share his many years of ministry experience and biblical knowledge to give us short but powerful devotional thoughts that will bless and encourage you each day.

Bible Booster Shots for the Believer is an innovative idea that is very well thought-out and organized to offer the believer what he or she needs to be strengthened in faith and built up in the ability to resist the devil so that he may flee. The booster shots cover everything for understanding that this life is based 100% on God's Word for living in victory, which comes from living 100% of God's Word.

Arnie Derksen's heart for the Word and love for the body of Christ is evident in the pages of this book. As he shares his insights and inspiration from the Scriptures, we receive great encouragement and a great blessing as we apply these truths in our lives.

Truly, I have grown to appreciate Rev. Derksen's passion and commitment in the few brief years that I have known him. His humility makes room for him as he allows God's leading and power to open doors and guide him as he ministers to the body of Christ either in song or in the Word, as this book so applies and displays.

It is with great honor and enthusiasm that I write this foreword and encourage you to read every page of this book because it will not only bless you, but it will strengthen you and build your faith.

God bless you as you read!

PREFACE

This work did not originally begin as a book. It has been a labor of my love for the Bible, the Word of God. One purpose in writing it was to bring balance into the arena of teaching on the subjects of prosperity and healing.

Whenever we choose to overemphasize one doctrine above the rest, we are heading for a lopsided Christianity. Obviously the message of salvation, the "good news" of the gospel, is of extreme importance in order for people to be saved. But consider this: most of the Bible was written to believers, the children of God, both in the Old Testament and the New Testament. Approximately 93–95% of the Bible was written about believers, to believers, and for believers. The Bible, God's Word, teaches us how to live as the children of God. God empowers us with the Holy Spirit to understand the Word, apply the Word, and LIVE according to His Word.

God, through Jesus Christ, His Son, provided the only way for souls to be saved. Jesus called it being "born again." God is not willing that any should perish, but that all should repent of sin and be saved, believing and receiving His Son. That is a one-time event. That is when true life begins. The question has been asked, "How should we then live?" The answer is found in the Bible.

1. ***CONFESS*** Jesus Christ as your Lord and Savior *(Romans 10: 9–10).*
2. ***BELIEVE*** that God raised Jesus Christ from the dead *(1 Corinthians 15: 1–6).*
3. Live a life of ***FAITH*** in God and His Word *(Romans 1:17).*
4. Be ***FILLED*** with the **HOLY SPIRIT** *(Ephesians 5:18).*
5. ***STUDY*** diligently the Word of God as your source of spiritual nutrition *(2 Timothy 2:15).*

6. Discipline your mind to live with an ***AWARENESS*** of **GOD'S PRESENCE** in your life *(1 Corinthians 15: 1–6).*
7. Above all, let ***GOD'S LOVE*** permeate every aspect, every word, and every action in your daily life *(1 Corinthians 13–* ***"Without LOVE, I AM NOTHING."****)*

INTRODUCTION

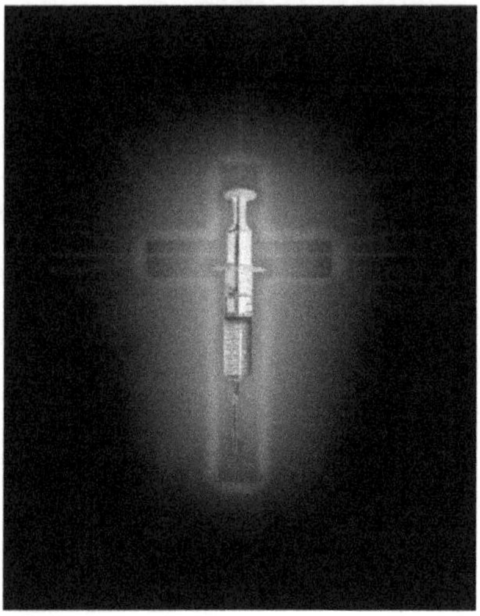

INTRODUCTION

A BOOST:

A boost is to push or shove up from below; to aid or assist toward progress or increase;

1. A push upwards
2. An increase in amount
3. An act that brings help or encouragement

A BOOSTER:

A booster is one (or something) that boosts;

1. An enthusiastic supporter
2. A supplementary dose of an immunizing agent to increase immunity

PRESCRIPTION:

For you to experience maximum benefits from these Bible boosters, they must first be digested mentally and then verbalized audibly and boldly with enthusiasm. When faith speaks, it is not timid or shy. A generous daily dose will drive away fear and cause the devil to flee. Two of Satan's tools are fear and torment. These "booster shots" have an eternal guarantee from GOD!

> *"For as the rain comes down, and the snow from heaven, and do not return there, but water the earth, and make it bring forth and bud, that it may give seed to the sower and bread to the eater, so shall MY WORD be that goes forth from MY MOUTH; IT SHALL NOT RETURN TO ME VOID,*

but IT SHALL ACCOMPLISH what I please, and IT SHALL PROSPER in the thing for which I SENT IT." (Isaiah 55:10–11)

BOOSTER SHOTS:

These Bible booster shots are based 100% on God's Word and on the biblical principle of CONFESSION. To confess literally means to "say with" or to "say the same thing." Applied to Scripture, it means to SAY THE SAME THING GOD SAYS ABOUT ME.

There are a negative and a positive side to confession. The negative side is those things I choose not to do or be anymore. The positive side is those things I desire to be and do. The negative side has to do with confessing our sins to God and turning away from them. The result is a positive one: (1) forgiveness of sin, (2) cleansing of sins, (3) the penalty of sin canceled, (4) the guilt of sin removed, and (5) becoming clean before God. Confession of sin makes me justified—just as if I had never sinned.

The first and most important step is this: I must agree with God that "ALL have sinned and fallen short of the glory of God" (Romans 3:23). That includes me. But praise God! His Word says, "If we confess our sins, He is FAITHFUL and JUST to FORGIVE us our sins and to cleanse us from all unrighteousness" (1 John 1:9). The cleansing agent is the BLOOD OF JESUS CHRIST (1 John 1:7).

The positive side of confession is to agree with God in ALL He says about the believer, His child, the "new creation" in Christ Jesus (2 Corinthians 5:17).

As a child of God, my Father, I must be willing to submit to Him and His Word. If my attitude is right and my heart is yielded to Him, I will pray with the psalmist in Psalm 139:23–24:

"Search me, O God, and know my heart; try me, and

> *know my anxieties; and see if there is any wicked way in me, and lead me in the way everlasting."*

Once the sin problem has been taken care of, the believer needs to learn to live with a "righteousness mentality" instead of a "sin mentality." For too many years, Christians have been more conscious of sin than of righteousness. For many centuries the preachers in the churches have majored in sin-consciousness. We have preached the law and kept our people under condemnation. Believers need to live with a righteousness mentality because Jesus Christ is OUR RIGHTEOUSNESS from God.

"But of Him you are in Christ Jesus, who became…" FOR US wisdom from God—and righteousness and sanctification and redemption--that, as IT IS WRITTEN, "He who glories, let him glory in the Lord" (1 Corinthians 1:30–31). "For He made Him who knew no sin to be sin FOR US, that WE might become the RIGHTEOUSNESS of GOD IN HIM" (2 Corinthians 5:21).

APPLICATION OF THE WORD

Most of the Bible is written in the second person. That is, it is written to YOU. Here is an example from Romans 10:9–10:

> *"That if YOU confess with YOUR mouth the Lord Jesus and believe in YOUR heart that God has raised Him from the dead, YOU will be saved. For with the heart ONE believes unto righteousness and with the MOUTH CONFESSION is made unto salvation."*

In order to make a simple and positive confession from that Scripture, substitute I for YOU and MY for YOUR. In other words, make a personal application of the Word of God. Be a doer of the Word and not only a hearer, deceiving yourself (James 1:22). Here is a simple and positive confession based on Romans 10:9–10:

"I confess with MY mouth that Jesus is Lord, and I believe in MY heart that God raised Him from the dead. Because of MY faith and confession, God says, I AM SAVED.

Here is another example of personal confession from 1 Thessalonians 5:23:

". . . and may YOUR whole spirit, soul, and body be preserved blameless at the coming of our LORD JESUS CHRIST."

By combining the two previous Scriptures, we can make the following confession:

"I confess that Jesus is Lord over MY spirit, over MY soul, and over MY body. I believe that God raised Him from the dead. By faith in MY heart I am justified, and by the confession of MY mouth I am saved. His resurrection power will keep ME blameless at His coming."

BE PREPARED FOR OPPOSITION

Be prepared for things to come against you when you make these confessions. Satan and the world do not want you to be victorious, joyful, prosperous, and healthy. The flesh will resist it also, because it is lazy when it comes to spiritual things. Always remember that FAITH is believing for something that has not yet taken place in your life. Many of these confessions have to be made by faith alone. Others may already be a present reality for you.

If you will just agree with God and not believe Satan, the world, or the flesh, you will have no problem making these confessions. These truths from God's Word must first become a reality in your spirit. Then, in due time, they will manifest themselves in the visible realm. Jesus said, "According to YOUR FAITH IT WILL BE DONE TO YOU."

Remember, to CONFESS means to verbally and audibly AGREE with God's Word. Begin to SAY the SAME thing about yourself that God SAYS about you. These confessions are powerful, and they will change your life if you consistently speak them. God's Word will produce what God intended it for. Are you willing to be a mighty instrument for God's glory and at the same time be a recipient of all the BLESSINGS of God?

The most effective method for using this book is to take one BOOSTER in the morning and prayerfully meditate on each of its seven ingredients. To further enhance the benefits of making these confessions, look up and read each Scripture noted. May you GROW in the GRACE and KNOWLEDGE of our Lord and Savior JESUS CHRIST the LIVING WORD.

BIBLE BOOSTER SHOTS

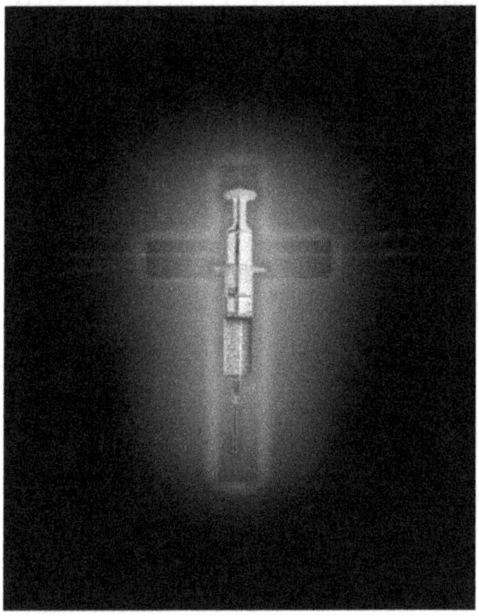

1st BOOSTER SHOT
100% GOD'S WORD

1) **GOD'S WAY IS PERFECT** *(Psalm 19:7)*

a. The Word of the Lord is PROVEN

b. He is a SHIELD for my PROTECTION *(Psalm 18:30)*

c. The law of the LORD is PERFECT *(Psalm 19:7)*

2) **THE WORD OF GOD REVIVES AND PRESERVES MY LIFE** *(Psalm 119:50)*

a. The Word of the LORD is ETERNAL *(Psalm 119:89)*

b. God's Word is FOREVER SETTLED in heaven

c. The Word of God is a LAMP to my feet *(Psalm 119:105)*

d. . . . and a LIGHT to my path

e. God's Word is TRUTH and RIGHTEOUSNESS *(Psalm 119:160)*

3) **THE WORD OF GOD IS LIVING AND POWERFUL** *(Hebrews 4:12)*

a. The Word of God is ACTIVE and EFFECTIVE

b. The Word of God is SHARPER than a TWO-EDGED SWORD

c. The Word of God pierces even to dividing soul and spirit

d. The Word of God discerns the thoughts and intents of the heart

e. The Word of God will accomplish that which God desires for my life. *(Isaiah 55:10–11)*

4) **ALL SCRIPTURE IS GOD-BREATHED** *(2 Timothy 3:16–17)*

a. It teaches me TRUTH

b. It CORRECTS me when I am wrong

c. It TRAINS me in RIGHTEOUSNESS

d. It EQUIPS me for every GOOD WORK

e. Scripture came through holy men of God as they were moved by the HOLY SPIRIT *(2 Peter 1:20–21)*

5) **GOD HAS MAGNIFIED ABOVE ALL THINGS HIS WORD AND HIS NAME** *(Psalm 138:2)*

a. God's Word has the POWER to keep me from sinning *(Psalm 119:11)*

b. The WORDS of the LORD are PURE, like silver purified in a furnace of earth, PURIFIED seven times *(Psalm 12:6)*

c. God has given Christ Jesus a NAME ABOVE EVERY NAME *(Philippians 2:9)*

6) **THE LIVING WORD OF GOD CREATED THE ENTIRE UNIVERSE** *(Genesis 1:1–31)*

a. "And GOD SAID . . ." These words are repeated nine times in Genesis 1.

b. By the Word of the LORD the heavens were made *(Psalm 33:6)*

c. By Jesus Christ, the SON OF GOD'S LOVE, all things were created . . . in heaven and on earth *(Colossians 1:16)*

d. God's Son upholds all things by the WORD OF HIS POWER *(Hebrews 1:3)*

7) **THE LORD IS WATCHING AND READY TO PERFORM HIS WORD** *(Jeremiah 1:12)*

   a. God promises to watch over His people *(Jeremiah 31:28)*
   b. Unless the LORD guards the city, the watchman stays awake in vain *(Psalm 127:1)*

2nd BOOSTER SHOT

ASSURANCE OF ETERNAL LIFE

1) **I HAVE RECEIVED JESUS AS MY LORD AND SAVIOR** *(John 1:12–13; John 3:3–8)*

- *a.* I believe in the Name of JESUS, God's Son
- *b.* God has given to me the POWER and RIGHT to become His child
- *c.* I am born again by the WILL of God
- *d.* I have gained entrance into the KINGDOM of GOD
- *e.* I am born again by the POWER of the WORD and the SPIRIT

2) **I BELIEVE IN JESUS CHRIST, GOD'S SON** *(John 3:15–18, 36; Romans 8:1)*

- *a.* God did not send His Son to condemn the world
- *b.* God sent His Son to SAVE THE WORLD
- *c.* I AM FREE FROM CONDEMNATION; I AM IN CHRIST JESUS

3) **I NOW HAVE ETERNAL LIFE** *(John 5:24; Ephesians 2:1–10)*

- *a.* I believe in the Son of God
- *b.* I have passed from death to LIFE
- *c.* I am SAVED by God's GRACE through FAITH
- *d.* I am NOT SAVED by my WORKS
- *e.* Salvation is a GIFT FROM GOD
- *f.* I am God's workmanship
- *g.* I am created in Christ Jesus to DO GOOD WORKS

4) **I CONTINUE TO FOLLOW THE WORDS OF JESUS CHRIST** *(John 8:31–36)*
   a. I live according to His WORD
   b. I am GROWING in His TRUTH
   c. His Truth sets me FREE from sin
   d. I am no longer a slave to sin
   e. The SON has set me FREE, and I am FREE indeed!

5) **I AM A CHILD OF GOD, LED BY HIS SPIRIT** *(Romans 8:14–17)*
   a. I have received the Spirit of SONSHIP
   b. I can rightfully claim God as MY FATHER
   c. I am an HEIR of God and a JOINT-HEIR with CHRIST

6) **I WALK IN THE LIGHT OF THE LIVING WORD OF GOD** *(1 John 1:7–10; 1 John 2:1–2)*
   a. I am blessed with fellowship in the FAMILY of GOD
   b. The BLOOD of JESUS CHRIST CLEANSES me from ALL sin
   c. I DO NOT have a SIN PROBLEM—I CONFESS MY SINS
   d. God is FAITHFUL and RIGHTEOUS—He forgives ALL my sins
   e. Jesus Christ is my ADVOCATE—He PAID for my sins COMPLETELY

7) **I KNOW I HAVE PASSED FROM DEATH TO LIFE** *(1 John 3:1–24)*
   a. Because I LOVE my brothers and sisters in the Lord
   b. I desire to SERVE my LORD
   c. I walk in His TRUTH
   d. I am LOOKING for HIS RETURN

3rd BOOSTER SHOT

BUILDING UP YOUR FAITH

(Hebrews 11:6)

1) **GOD HAS GIVEN ME "A MEASURE OF FAITH"** *(Romans 12:3)*

   a. FAITH is like a SEED that GROWS *(Matthew 17:20)*

   b. My heart is like the soil that receives the WORD *(Mark 4:13–20)*

   c. My mouth is the sower that plants the seed *(Matthew 13:18–23)*

   d. Faith grows as I listen to and obey the WORD *(Romans 10:17)*

2) **I KEEP LOOKING TO JESUS** *(Hebrews 12:2)*

   a. Jesus is the AUTHOR and FINISHER of my FAITH

   b. His eyes are on me *(1 Peter 3:12)*

   c. His ears are open to my prayers *(1 Peter 3:12)*

3) **I WALK BY FAITH—NOT BY SIGHT** *(2 Corinthians 5:7)*

   a. I do not depend on my feelings

   b. I am not moved by circumstances

   c. I am guided by GOD'S WORD *(Psalm 119:105)*

4) **GOD HAS GIVEN ME A SPIRIT OF POWER, OF LOVE, and OF A SOUND MIND** *(2 Timothy 1:7)*

   a. God has not given me a spirit of fear

   b. I LIVE in God's PERFECT LOVE *(1 John 4:18)*

   c. I have NO FEAR in GOD'S LOVE

   d. I will exercise my FAITH through LOVE *(Galatians 5:6)*

5) **THE LORD IS THE STRENGTH OF MY LIFE** *(Psalm 27:1)*

a. I am STRONG in the LORD and in His POWER *(Ephesians 6:10)*

b. I CAN DO ALL THINGS through Christ *(Philippians 4:13)*

c. God will supply ALL my needs *(Philippians 4:19)*

6) **GOD ALWAYS LEADS ME IN TRIUMPHANT VICTORY IN CHRIST JESUS** *(2 Corinthians 2:14)*

a. I TRUST in the LORD and I AM SAFE (Proverbs 29:25)

b. I am born of GOD and I OVERCOME the world (1 John 5:4)

c. The VICTORY is in my FAITH in CHRIST JESUS

7) **I HAVE AUTHORITY AND POWER TO TRAMPLE ON THE ENEMY** *(Luke 10:19)*

a. Nothing shall by any means hurt me

b. I am not afraid of man or demons

c. GREATER IS HE THAT IS IN ME than he that is in the world *(1 John 4:4)*

d. JESUS IS MY LORD!

4th BOOSTER SHOT

DEFEATING WORRY AND FEAR

1) **I AM BORN OF THE SPIRIT OF GOD** *(1 John 4:1–6)*
   a. I am a NEW CREATION in Christ *(2 Corinthians 5:17)*
   b. I OVERCOME the world, Satan, and the flesh *(1 John 4:1–16)*
   c. I am MORE than a CONQUEROR through Christ *(Romans 8:37)*

2) **I AM A MEMBER IN THE BODY OF CHRIST** *(1 Corinthians 12:27)*
   a. I will NOT worry, I will OBEY JESUS *(Matthew 6:25)*
   b. I will NOT fear, because GOD is WITH ME *(Isaiah 41:10)*
   c. I will NOT be ANXIOUS, GOD ANSWERS PRAYER *(Philippians 4:6)*

3) **I WILL FEAR NO EVIL, THE LORD IS MY SHEPHERD** *(Psalm 23)*
   a. I shall not be in want of anything
   b. HE restores my soul with wisdom and clear thinking *(Proverbs 2:6)*
   c. The Word of God and the HOLY SPIRIT COMFORT me
   d. Goodness and mercy follow me

4) **NO WEAPON FORMED AGAINST ME WILL PREVAIL OR PROSPER** *(Isaiah 54:17)*
   a. Oppression and fear cannot come near me *(Isaiah 54:14)*
   b. I am established in the righteousness of God
   c. I have NOTHING TO FEAR

5) **MY LIFE IS IN THE SHELTER OF THE MOST HIGH GOD** *(Psalm 91)*
   a. I am safe in the presence of God
   b. He said, "I WILL NEVER LEAVE YOU OR FORSAKE YOU" *(Hebrews 13:5)*
   c. The LORD will DELIVER me out of all afflictions *(Psalm 34:19)*
   d. The Lord has commanded His angels to guard me in all my ways

6) **I AM BEING RESCUED FROM THIS PRESENT EVIL AGE** *(Galatians 1:4)*
   a. Christ GAVE Himself for my sins
   b. He has delivered me from the guilt and penalty of sin
   c. . . . according to the will of God My FATHER

7) **I DO NOT WASTE TIME WORRYING OR FRETTING IN FEAR** *(Psalm 37:1–9)*
   a. I TRUST in the LORD and DO GOOD
   b. I DO NOT envy the workers of iniquity
   c. I dwell in the land and ENJOY God's PROTECTION
   d. I delight myself in the LORD, and He blesses me
   e. I commit my life to the LORD, I TRUST in Him
   f. The PEACE of God GUARDS my heart and mind *(Philippians 4:7)*

5th BOOSTER SHOT
LIVING IN HEALTH

1) **I AM HEALED BY THE WORD OF GOD** *(Psalm 107:20)*
   a. I am DELIVERED from the enemy's destructions
   b. The LORD FORGIVES all my iniquities *(Psalm 103:3)*
   c. The LORD HEALS all my diseases

2) **JESUS IS MY HEALER** *(Matthew 8:17 and Isaiah 53)*
   a. He took my infirmities
   b. He bore my sicknesses
   c. He was wounded for my transgressions *(Isaiah 53:5)*
   d. By His stripes I am HEALED

3) **I BELIEVE IN THE GIFTS OF THE HOLY SPIRIT** *(1 Corinthians 12:4–11)*
   a. I receive the "GIFTS OF HEALINGS" *(1 Corinthians 12:9)*
   b. The Son of Righteousness has arisen with HEALING IN HIS WINGS *(Malachi 4:2)*

4) **I LISTEN CAREFULLY TO THE WORD OF GOD** *(Exodus 15:26)*
   a. I do what is RIGHT in His sight
   b. I walk in OBEDIENCE to God's Word
   c. The Lord is the One who HEALS me

5) **THE SAME SPIRIT THAT RAISED CHRIST FROM THE DEAD DWELLS IN ME** *(Romans 8:11)*

a. The Holy Spirit resides in my mortal body
b. The Holy Spirit is a HEALTHY SPIRIT
c. The same CREATIVE SPIRIT of God that hovered over the face of the waters dwells in me *(Genesis 1:2)*

6) **I BELIEVE THAT SIGNS WILL FOLLOW THOSE WHO BELIEVE** *(Mark 16:17–18)*

a. In the NAME OF JESUS they will drive out demons
b. They will speak with new tongues
c. They will lay hands on the sick and THEY WILL RECOVER
d. I AM A BELIEVER

7) **MY TONGUE HAS THE POWER OF LIFE AND DEATH** *(Proverbs 18:21)*

a. I choose LIFE this day *(Joshua 24:15)*
b. I speak words of LIFE-GIVING substance in FAITH *(Hebrews 11:1)*
c. I speak words of HEALING

6th BOOSTER SHOT
LIVING IN GOD'S PROSPERITY

1) **CHRIST HAS REDEEMBED ME FROM THE CURSE OF PROVERTY** *(2 Corinthians 8:9; Galatians 3:13–14)*

   a. For death He has given me ETERNAL LIFE *(John 5:24)*
   b. For sickness He has given me HEALTH *(1 Peter 2:24)*
   c. For poverty He has given me WEALTH *(Proverbs 10:15; Proverbs 10:22)*

2) **I GIVE TO THE LORD ACCORDING TO HIS WORD** *(Malachi 3:8–11)*

   a. I GIVE in obedience to God, and God ALWAYS rewards OBEDIENCE
   b. The promise of God is to pour out a BLESSING. There will not be room enough to receive it.
   c. There will be "food" or resources for God's work
   d. God says He will REBUKE the devourer for my sake. Satan himself cannot stop it.

3) **WITH THE MEASURE I GIVE IT WILL BE MEASURED BACK TO ME** *(Luke 6:38)*

   a. God gives a GOOD (honest, just, pleasing, acceptable, excellent . . .) measure
   b. "Pressed down"—there are no air pockets in God's measure
   c. "Shaken together"—God will not, cannot shortchange anybody

d. "Running over"—the SUPERABUNDANCE of God's GRACE

4) **I SOW BOUNTIFULLY, THEREFORE I REAP BOUNTIFULLY** *(2 Corinthians 9:6–11)*

a. I GIVE cheerfully, and God's GRACE abounds to me

b. God promises that I will have abundance for every good work

c. God will supply and increase my "storehouse" (bank account)

d. God will multiply the "seeds" I have sown

e. God will enrich me so that I can be GENEROUS in every opportunity with THANKSGIVING to God

5) **I PROSPER UNDER THE TEACHING AND PREACHING OF GOD'S WORD** *(Romans 10:17)*

a. My FAITH GROWS through consistently HEARING God's Word

b. I AGREE with what God says

c. If I LIVE in OBEDIENCE to God's Word, the Lord will grant me ABUNDANT PROSPERITY *(Deuteronomy 28:1–14; Job 36:11)*

6) **WHATEVER I DO WILL PROSPER** *(Psalm 1:1–3)*

a. I do not walk in the counsel of the ungodly

b. I do not stand in agreement with sinners

c. I do not participate with the scornful or cynical

d. I DELIGHT in reading God's Word

e. I meditate in the Word, dwell on it—think on it always

f. I am like a tree planted by the RIVERS of water

g. . . . will produce an ABUNDANT HARVEST

7) **GOD WILL SUPPLY ALL MY NEEDS**
(Philippians 4:19; Psalm 23:1)

a. . . . according to His RICHES in GLORY by Christ Jesus

b. The Lord (Creator, Sustainer, Owner of the Universe) can and will provide so that I SHALL NOT WANT for anything

7th BOOSTER SHOT
DOMINION OVER SIN

1) **I AM MORE THAN A CONQUEROR THROUGH CHRIST WHO LOVED ME** *(Romans 8:37–39)*

- *a.* "More than"—over and above; super victorious; overpowering in achieving abundant VICTORY
- *b.* I am convinced that nothing shall be able to separate me from the LOVE of GOD which is in Christ Jesus OUR LORD
- *c.* He who is IN ME is GREATER than he who is in the world *(1 John 4:4)*

2) **I HAVE BEEN CRUCIFIED WITH CHRIST—I HAVE DIED TO SIN** *(Galatians 2:20)*

- *a.* Christ LIVES in me
- *b.* CHRIST LOVES ME . . . He gave Himself for me
- *c.* I do not let sin rule in my mortal body *(Romans 6:2–4)*
- *d.* I am no longer a slave to sin *(Romans 6:22)*

3) **I HAVE BEEN SET FREE FROM SIN** *(Romans 6:22)*

- *a.* By choice I am a bondservant of Christ *(Ephesians 6:6)* and of God's RIGHTEOUSNESS *(Romans 6:22)*
- *b.* The fruit of righteous living is HOLINESS

4) **I AM BORN OF GOD AND I AM AN OVERCOMER** *(1 John 5:4)*

- *a.* Whatever is BORN OF GOD overcomes the world (the secular system under the influence and control of Satan)
- *b.* My VICTORY is assured when I WALK BY FAITH
- *c.* I believe that JESUS IS THE SON OF GOD

5) **I LIVE BY THE SPIRIT OF GOD** *(Galatians 5:16–25)*

a. I walk in the SPIRIT—I DO NOT fulfill the lust of the flesh
b. I am led by the SPIRIT into the realm of VICTORY
c. The works of the flesh are EVIDENT (recognizable, visible, tiring)
d. The FRUIT of the Spirit is LOVE (let it grow; nurture it)

6) **MY LIFE IS FULLY COMMITTED TO THE LORD** *(Proverbs 16:3)*

a. He establishes my thought-life through His WORD
b. I am being TRANSFORMED by the renewing of my mind *(Romans 12:2)*
c. I CAN DO all things THROUGH CHRIST who STRENGTHENS ME *(Philippians 4:13)*

7) **IN THE NAME OF JESUS I PUSH BACK THE ENEMY—SIN—and TRAMPLE ON MY ADVERSARY** *(Psalm 44:5)*

a. God will CRUSH Satan under my feet *(Romans 16:20; Genesis 3:15)*
b. Jesus has given me AUTHORITY to trample on serpents and scorpions, and over all the power of the enemy, and nothing shall by any means hurt me *(Luke 10:19)*
c. JESUS IS MY LORD; I BELONG TO HIM; HE FIGHTS MY BATTLES FOR ME. BY FAITH I STAND AND SEE THE SALVATION OF THE LORD.

8th BOOSTER SHOT
SUCCESSFUL LIVING

1) **JESUS CAME TO BRING A MORE ABUNDANT LIFE** *(John 10:10)*
    a. JESUS is the Author (Originator) and Finisher (Perfecter) of my faith *(Hebrews 12:2)*
    b. JESUS took my failure and defeat, nailed it to the CROSS, and disarmed the enemies of BELIEVERS . . . triumphing over them *(Colossians 2:13–15)*

2) **THE WORD OF GOD CAUSES ME TO BE PROSPEROUS AND SUCCESSFUL** *(Joshua 1:7–8)*
    a. I study, meditate in, and observe the WORD OF GOD so that I may PROSPER wherever I go and whatever I do
    b. God says I will have GOOD SUCCESS
    c. I am STRONG and COURAGEOUS in the POWER of the HOLY SPIRIT *(Acts 1:8)*
    d. My SUCCESS in GOD serves as a WITNESS to the world *(Acts 1:8b)*

3) **THE BLESSINGS OF ABRAHAM ARE MINE THROUGH FAITH IN JESUS CHRIST** *(Galatians 3:14; Genesis 12:3)*
    a. My circumcision is of the heart, by the Spirit *(Romans 2:28–29)*
    b. I am a Jew inwardly, because I have received the TRUE MESSIAH, Jesus Christ the LORD
    c. True Judaism is found in those who are righteous before God, regardless of ethnic or religious background ("Judaism" means TRUE PRAISE)

4) **I COMMIT WHATEVER I DO TO THE LORD, AND MY PLANS SUCCEED** *(Proverbs 16:3)*

a. I delight myself in the Lord, and He gives me the desires of my heart *(Psalm 37:4)*

b. I commit my life to the Lord, I TRUST in Him, and He brings it to pass *(Psalm 37:5)*

c. I REST in the Lord and wait patiently for His LEADING *(Psalm 37:7–9)*

d. My TOTAL SALVATION is of the Lord *(Psalm 37:39–40)*

5) **IF I CAREFULLY FOLLOW AND OBEY GOD'S WORD, ALL HIS BLESSINGS COME UPON ME** *(Deuteronomy 28:1–14)*

a. I have POWER to be OBEDIENT because I am born of God *(1 John 5:1–5)*

b. The Holy Spirit of God dwells in me *(1 Corinthians 6:19)*

c. My body is the temple of the HOLY SPIRIT

6) **I CAST (ROLL) MY BURDEN (CARES) ON THE LORD, AND HE SUSTAINS ME** *(Psalm 55:22)*

a. God really CARES for me *(1 Peter 5:7)*

b. He will not let me fail

c. All my anxieties, distractions, burdens, and worries are not worth worrying about because the FATHER's LOVE provides both my daily needs and my special needs

7) **I AM SUCCESSFUL IN OVERCOMING THE WORLD** *(1 John 5:4)*

a. The VICTORY that overcomes the world is found in my steadfast FAITH in JESUS CHRIST—He was VICTORIOUS *(John 16:33)*

b. I overcome evil with good *(Romans 12:21)*

9th BOOSTER SHOT
DEFENSE AGAINST SATANIC ATTACKS

1) **I PUT ON THE BELT OF TRUTH** *(Ephesians 6:14)*
   a. The living Word of God is TRUTH *(John 17:17)*
   b. I am sanctified by the Word
   c. The TRUTH sets me FREE *(John 8:32)*
   d. JESUS is the Way, the TRUTH, and the Life *(John 14:6)*

2) **I PUT ON THE BREASTPLATE OF RIGHTEOUSNESS** *(Ephesians 6:14b)*
   a. Jesus Christ is my RIGHTEOUSNESS *(2 Corinthians 5:21)*
   b. Christ became sin for me that I might become the RIGHTEOUSNESS of God in Christ
   c. I REFUSE to accept any CONDEMNATION from Satan *(Romans 8:1)*

3) **I FIT MY FEET WITH THE GOSPEL OF PEACE** *(Ephesians 6:15)*
   a. JESUS is the PRINCE OF PEACE *(Isaiah 9:6; Acts 3:15; Acts 5:31)*
   b. I have GOOD NEWS to share—JESUS is the ANSWER *(1 Peter 3:15)*
   c. I let the PEACE of God RULE in my heart *(Colossians 3:15)*

4) **I LIFT UP THE SHIELD OF FAITH** *(Ephesians 6:16)*
   a. With the shield of faith I extinguish the flaming arrows of the evil one
   b. I spoil all of Satan's plans for my destruction *(Colossians 2:15)*

   c. The Sovereign Lord Himself is my SHIELD *(Genesis 15:1; Psalm 3:3)*

5) **I PUT ON THE HELMET OF SALVATION** *(Ephesians 6:17)*
   a. I set my mind on things above, not on earthly things *(Colossians 3:2)*
   b. I do not conform any longer to the PATTERN of this world *(Romans 12:2)*
   c. I am being TRANSFORMED by the RENEWING of my mind *(Romans 12:2b)*
   d. The helmet of SALVATION protects my mind

6) **I TAKE THE SWORD OF THE SPIRIT—THE WORD OF GOD** *(Ephesians 6:17)*
   a. I will speak the WORD in season and out of season *(2 Timothy 4:2)*
   b. I will fill my heart with the WORD of GOD *(Psalm 119:11)*
   c. The WORD of God is the ammunition that empowers my mouth like a sword

7) **I WILL PRAY IN THE SPIRIT ON ALL OCCASIONS** *(Ephesians 6:18)*
   a. I will not be anxious about anything *(Philippians 4:6)*
   b. I will maintain a constant attitude of prayer *(1 Thessalonians 5:17)*
   c. I will pray with thanksgiving in my heart *(Philippians 4:6)*
   d. I will pray in the Spirit and with understanding *(2 Corinthians 14:13–15)*

10th BOOSTER SHOT
FULLNESS OF THE SPIRIT

1) **I AM FILLED WITH THE HOLY SPIRIT OF GOD** *(Ephesians 5:18)*
   a. The Holy Spirit is in CONTROL of my life (whatever my heart is filled with will control my life)
   b. He has given me a heavenly prayer language *(1 Corinthians 14:1–19)*
   c. He has filled me with a RIVER OF JOY flowing out of my innermost being *(John 7:38)*
   d. He gives me POWER to speak the Word of God BOLDLY *(Acts 1:8)*

2) **I HAVE RECEIVED AN ANOINTING FROM THE HOLY SPIRIT** *(1 John 2:20, 27)*
   a. That anointing is in me and it remains
   b. The HOLY SPIRIT is a Person, and I am determined not to *"quench"* Him, not to "grieve" Him, and never to ignore Him *(Ephesians 4:30; 1 Thessalonians 5:19)*
   c. The Spirit GUIDES me into all TRUTH and GLORIFIES JESUS CHRIST *(John 16:13–15)*

3) **THE HOLY SPIRIT IS MY COMFORTER AND COUNSELOR** *(John 14:16)*
   a. The Holy Spirit is my HELPER—He will ABIDE FOREVER
   b. He is the Spirit of TRUTH and testifies of JESUS *(John 15:26)*

4) **THE HOLY SPIRIT LEADS ME BECAUSE I AM A CHILD OF GOD** *(Romans 8:14–16)*

a. I did not receive a spirit of bondage that leads to fear
b. I received the Spirit of son ship
c. I can rightfully call God my Father
d. The Spirit Himself bears witness that I am a child of God

5) **I AM STRENGTHED BY THE HOLY SPIRIT IN MY INNER BEING** *(Ephesians 3:16)*

a. He causes Christ to dwell in my heart by faith *(Ephesians 5:17)*
b. I am being rooted and grounded in LOVE
c. He teaches me to know the LOVE OF CHRIST
d. He teaches beyond human knowledge in order to FILL me with the FULLNESS of GOD

6) **BY THE POWER OF THE HOLY SPIRIT I CONFESS THAT JESUS IS LORD** *(1 Corinthians 12:3)*

a. The Holy Spirit empowers me to GLORIFY GOD in word and deed

7) **I BELIEVE IN THE GIFTS OF THE HOLY SPIRIT** *(1 Corinthians 12:7–11)*

a. The Word of WISDOM = the ability to use knowledge correctly (application)
b. The Word of KNOWLEDGE = revelation of information for a specific purpose
c. Supernatural FAITH = goes beyond saving faith: TOTAL TRUST and NO DOUBT
d. GIFTS of HEALINGS = the plural indicates many kinds of disorders
e. Working of MIRACLES = going beyond the ordinary course of natural law
f. PROPHECY = divine disclosures, edifying revelation, exhortation, comfort

g. DISCERNING of spirits = understanding the spirit world; truth and error
h. TONGUES = unknown tongues in different forms
i. INTERPRETATION of TONGUES = being able to translate tongues so everyone benefits

> *"But one and the same Spirit works all these things, distributing to each one individually as HE WILLS."*
> *(1 Corinthians 12:11)*

11th BOOSTER SHOT
RENEWING THE MIND

1) **I DO NOT CONFORM TO THE THINKING PATTERNS OF THIS WORLD** *(Romans 12:1–2)*

a. I present my physical body as a living sacrifice to God

b. To live holy and acceptable to God, is a spiritual act of worship

c. I am being transformed as I renew my mind with godly thinking:

i. A power that transforms my thoughts, which lead to formulating . . .My purpose in life that will proceed to dictate my actions

ii. My actions become character-determining habits . . .Which shape my life and set the course for my future

d. The path to godly living is not complicated:

i. It is not energized by the flesh

ii. But it calls me to a willing submission to the Father's provision and ways

e. As a result, I am able to test and prove that good and acceptable and perfect will of God.

2) **I AM WHAT I THINK** *(Proverbs 23:7)*

a. My mind is like a computer (my thoughts determine my actions)

b. God has the power and ability to put information in our minds *(Jeremiah 31:33)*

c. Jesus commanded me to "love the LORD my God with ALL my MIND" *(Mark 12:30)*

MIND — (Greek dianoia) *literally "a thinking through." The word suggests understanding, insight, meditation, reflection, perception, faculty of thought. When this faculty is renewed by the Holy Spirit the whole mindset changes from the fearful negativism of the carnal mind to the vibrant, positive thinking of the spiritually alive mind.*

d. The resurrected, glorified Christ searches the MINDS and hearts. *(Revelation 2:23)*

3) **OUT OF THE OVERFLOW OF MY HEART MY MOUTH SPEAKS** *(Matthew 12:34–37)*

a. My heart is the storage place of all thoughts and knowledge recorded in my mind

b. I choose to store up good and righteous things in my heart

c. If my heart is full of good treasures, I will speak good things

4) **I HAVE THE MIND OF CHRIST** *(1 Corinthians 2:16)*

a. I am being renewed in the spirit of my mind *(Ephesians 4:23)*

b. I let the mind of Christ work in me mightily *(Colossians 1:29)*

5) **I DISCIPLINE MY THOUGHT LIFE AND EXERCISE MY POWER OF CHOICE** *(Philippians 4:8)*

a. I choose to think on things that are TRUE, NOBLE, JUST, PURE, LOVELY, OF GOOD REPORT, EXCELLENT, and PRAISEWORTHY

b. I reject all thoughts that cannot pass this test

6) **I SET MY MIND ON THINGS ABOVE** *(Colossians 3:1–4)*
   a. I choose to think on the WORD OF GOD—spiritual and eternal truths
   b. I do not dwell on worldly things for pleasure or fleshly pursuits
   c. My life is now hidden with Christ in God
   d. When Christ APPEARS in His fullness of glory, I will also appear with Him in glory

7) **I AM CLEAR-MINDED AND SELF-CONTROLLED** *(2 Peter 5:8)*
   a. The devil has no power over me when I have the MIND OF CHRIST
   b. He may roar like a lion, but I will ignore him and he must flee *(James 4:7–10)*

12th BOOSTER SHOT
CULTIVATING THE FRUIT OF THE SPIRIT

1) **I AM A BRANCH IN THE TRUE VINE** *(John 15:1–5)*

   a. I am a Spirit-filled believer, producing spiritual fruit
   b. By myself I can do nothing
   c. Through Christ and the Holy Spirit I can do all things *(Philippians 4:13)*

2) **THE HOLY SPIRIT IS PRODUCING FRUIT IN MY REGENERATED HUMAN SPIRIT** *(John 3:6–7; Galatians 5:22, 25; and John 15: 1–5)*

   a. God established an unchanging principle in Genesis 1:12: ALL seeds reproduce according to their kind
   b. Likewise, the Holy Spirit produces fruit from Himself in my spirit

3) **THE FRUIT OF THE SPIRIT IS LOVE** *(Galatians 5:22–23)*

   a. JOY is LOVE'S strength *(Nehemiah 8:10)*
   b. PEACE is LOVE'S security *(John 14:27; Philippians 4:7)*
   c. LONGSUFFERING (patience) is LOVE'S endurance *(Romans 5:3–5; Ephesians 4:2)*
   d. KINDNESS is LOVE'S conduct *(1 Corinthians 13:4–7)*
   e. GOODNESS is LOVE'S character *(Matthew 7:17; Matthew 19:17; Psalm 27:13)*
   f. FAITHFULNESS is LOVE'S confidence *(Matthew 25:21; Psalm 89:1–8)*
   g. GENTLENESS is LOVE'S humility *(Matthew 11:29; Philippians 2:8)*
   h. SELF-CONTROL is LOVE'S VICTORY *(1 Peter 1:5–11)*

4) **THE HEART OF GOD IS LOVE** *(John 3:16)*
   a. God so loved the world that He GAVE
   b. With God's LOVE in my heart I have a desire to KEEP ON GIVING
   c. I LOVE the Lord my God; I LOVE my neighbor as myself *(Matthew 23:37–40)*

5) **I FOLLOW THE WAY OF LOVE** *(1 Corinthians 13)*
   a. LOVE never fails
   b. Without LOVE I am nothing . . . my works profit me nothing *(1 Corinthians 13:2–3)*
   c. I pursue LOVE as my number-one priority *(1 Corinthians 14:1)*

6) **I HAVE GREAT PEACE BECAUSE I LOVE THE WORD OF GOD** *(Psalm 119:165)*
   a. The Word of God has given me LIFE *(Psalm 119:50)*
   b. The Word of God is PURE, and I LOVE it *(Psalm 119:140)*

7) **I LET THE PEACE OF GOD RULE IN MY HEART** *(Colossians 3:15)*
   a. I let the Word of Christ DWELL in me richly *(Colossians 3:16)*
   b. I have the MIND OF CHRIST *(1 Corinthians 2:16)*
   c. The Holy Spirit produces spiritual fruit in my life

13th BOOSTER SHOT
ACCESS INTO GOD'S PRESENCE

1) **I HAVE GAINED ACCESS THROUGH THE LORD JESUS CHRIST** *(Romans 5:2)*

a. By FAITH in Him, He has opened the door to God's GRACE

b. I REJOICE in the hope of the glory of God

c. By FAITH I STAND in this GRACE—surrounded by it

2) **I HAVE ENTERED INTO THIS BLESSING THROUGH THE MAIN DOOR** *(John 10:9)*

a. Jesus alone is the MAIN DOOR—He said, "I AM THE DOOR"

b. Having entered in through the DOOR, I AM SAVED

c. Once I entered through the DOOR, Christ entered into my heart

3) **I NOW HAVE ACCESS TO THE THRONE OF GRACE** *(Hebrews 4:16)*

a. I can come boldly, without reservation

b. I don't need fancy words, I can simply ask for help

c. This is not a throne of judgment, but of grace

d. I find MERCY for the past and GRACE for the present and the future

4) **I HAVE ACCESS TO THE FATHER BY THE HOLY SPIRIT** *(Ephesians 2:18–19)*

a. I am no longer a stranger or foreigner

b. I am a fellow citizen with the saints

c. I am a member of the HOUSEHOLD OF GOD

5) **I HAVE BOLDNESS AND ACCESS THROUGH FAITH IN CHRIST JESUS MY LORD** *(Ephesians 3:11–12)*

a. I have ACCESS with CONFIDENCE

b. I keep my heart pure to maintain confidence toward God (1 John 3:18–23)

c. Trusting God comes through FAITH IN CHRIST (2 Corinthians 3:4)

6) **I ENTER INTO GOD'S PRESENCE WITH THANKGIVING AND PRAISE** *(Psalm 100:4)*

a. God inhabits the PRAISES of His people *(Psalm 22:3)*

b. The PRESENCE of God's kingdom power is directly related to the practice of God's PRAISE

c. Wherever God's people exalt His name, He is ready to manifest His kingdom power in the way most appropriate to the situation as His rule is invited to invade our setting

d. PRAISE prepares a specific and present place for God among His people

e. God awaits the prayerful and praise-filled worship of His people as an ENTRY POINT for His KINGDOM to come—to enter—that HIS "will be done" in human circumstances *(Luke 11:2–4)*

7) **I CAN STAND CLEAN BEFORE GOD** *(1 Corinthians 6:11)*

a. I am washed, sanctified, and justified in the NAME of the LORD JESUS and by the SPIRIT of our God

b. I have been REDEEMED to God by the BLOOD of the Lamb *(Revelation 5:9)*

c. I have been brought near to God by the BLOOD of Christ *(Ephesians 2:13)*

14th BOOSTER SHOT
LIVING IN VICTORY

1) **I HAVE DIED TO SIN—I CAN NO LONGER LIVE IN IT** *(Romans 2–7)*

a. By faith I have been united to Christ in His death
b. By faith I have been united to Christ in His resurrection
c. My old self was crucified with Him (crucifixion is death)
d. That old body—system—of sin was rendered inoperative
e. I am no longer a slave to sin
f. When I died to sin, I was SET FREE from sin!

2) **I HAVE BEEN CRUCIFIED WITH CHRIST** *(Galatians 2:20)*

a. It is no longer the old "I" that lives
b. Christ now lives in me and through me in my personality
c. This new life I live in the same body of flesh
d. I now live by faith in the SON OF GOD
e. The SON OF GOD loved me and GAVE HIMSELF for me

3) **I PRESENT MY BODY AS A LIVING SACRIFICE** *(Romans 12:1–2)*

a. My desire is to live HOLY, ACCEPTABLE to God
b. This is only reasonable in light of the SACRIFICE that was made for me
c. I no longer conform to this world and its philosophy
d. I am being TRANSFORMED by the RENEWING of my mind through the WORD of GOD

e. As a result I can prove what is that GOOD and ACCEPTABLE and PERFECT WILL OF GOD in my daily life through the RENEWING power of the Holy Spirit (Titus 3:5)

4) **MY BODY IS THE TEMPLE OF THE HOLY SPIRIT** *(1 Corinthians 6:19–20)*

a. I have been redeemed with the precious BLOOD OF THE LAMB of God

b. God dwells in me by His Holy Spirit

c. Therefore it is only reasonable to GLORIFY GOD in my body and my spirit

5) **THERE IS VICTORY IN THE CROSS OF JESUS** *(Galatians 6:14)*

a. By the CROSS the world has been crucified TO ME

b. The world has become death to me—I no longer live in or for dead things

c. The CROSS is an instrument of death (Matthew 10:38)

d. My CROSS is to die daily to self and LIVE for Christ

6) **I HAVE PUT ON THE NEW SELF** *(Ephesians 4:24; Colossians 3:10)*

a. My new self is created according to God in true righteousness and holiness

b. My new self is being renewed in knowledge in the image of its Creator

c. I have taken OFF the old self with all of its sinful practices

7) **I THANK GOD HE GIVES ME VICTORY THROUGH JESUS CHRIST** *(1 Corinthians 15: 57–58)*

a. I stand firm and steadfast, letting nothing move me

b. I give myself fully to the work of the Lord

c. I know that my labor is not in vain in the Lord

15th BOOSTER SHOT
GUARDING INNER PEACE

1) **I HAVE PEACE WITH GOD THROUGH THE LORD JESUS CHRIST** *(Romans 5:1)*

   a. I have been declared righteous through FAITH in Jesus Christ
   b. I have been justified by His BLOOD *(Romans 5:9–10)*
   c. I am SAVED from the wrath of God through Christ
   d. I have been RECONCILED (restored to relationship) to God through Christ's death
   e. I am SAVED by His resurrection POWER

2) **THE PEACE OF GOD IS GUARDING MY HEART AND MIND IN CHRIST JESUS** *(Philippians 4:7)*

   a. I refuse to be anxious about anything *(Philippians 4:6)*
   b. I choose not to worry
   c. I choose to make my requests known to God
   d. By faith, I will add THANKSGIVING to my PRAYER and petitions

3) **THE GOD OF PEACE IS WITH ME** *(Philippians 4:9)*

   a. That which I RECEIVE AND LEARN, I will appropriate into my life
   b. The PROMISE is that the GOD OF PEACE will be with me

4) **I LET THE PEACE OF GOD RULE IN MY HEART** *(Colossians 3:15–16)*

   a. I am a member of one body—the BODY OF CHRIST
   b. I am THANKFUL for this membership

   c. I let the Word of Christ dwell in me richly
   d. With GRACE in my heart, I will sing in psalms and hymns and spiritual songs

5) **I HAVE GREAT PEACE, BECAUSE I LOVE THE WORD OF GOD** *(Psalm 119:165)*
   a. The Word removes the stumbling blocks
   b. It changes stumbling blocks into STEPPING STONES
   c. God's PEACE is so GREAT, it passes natural understanding *(Philippians 4:7)*

6) **THE LORD HAS BLESSED ME WITH HIS PEACE** *(Psalm 29:11)*
   a. His PEACE gives me strength and health and well-being
   b. PEACE, from the HEBREW *shalom,* is abundant in blessing, with WHOLENESS, COMPLETENESS, UNBROKENNESS, FULL HEALTH, TOTAL WELL-BEING, and SOUNDNESS IN EVERY WAY

7) **JESUS HAS GIVEN ME HIS PEAC*E*** *(John 14:27)*
   a. He left it with me
   b. He will never take it back
   c. It is not a temporary PEACE like the world gives
   d. I refuse to allow trouble into my heart
   e. With the PEACE of GOD given me by Jesus, I AM NOT AFRAID

16th BOOSTER SHOT
THE POWER OF GOD'S LOVE

1) **GOD SO LOVED THE WORLD THAT HE GAVE HIS ONLY BEGOTTEN SON** *(John 3:16)*
    - *a.* God's love is unconditional LOVE, LOVE by choice, an act of the will
    - *b.* God's love is unconquerable benevolence and undefeatable goodwill
    - *c.* God's love (Greek: *agapao,* a verb) will never seek anything but the highest good for mankind
    - *d.* God's love (Greek: *agape,* a " – noun) is God's unconditional LOVE
    - *e.* The Son of God LOVES ME and GAVE Himself for me *(Galatians 2:20)*
    - *f.* I believe and I receive GOD'S LOVE

2) **I AM CONVINCED THAT *NOTHING* CAN SEPARATE ME FROM GOD'S LOVE** *(Romans 8:38–39)*
    - *a.* This LOVE is in Christ Jesus my LORD
    - *b.* Neither death nor life, angels nor demons, the present nor the future nor any powers, height nor depth, nor anything else will be able to separate me from the LOVE of God
    - *c.* I am more than a conqueror through Him who LOVED me

3) **GOD HAS POURED OUT HIS LOVE INTO MY HEART BY THE HOLY SPIRIT:** *(Romans 5:5–8)*
    - *a.* When I was still without strength, Christ died for me
    - *b.* At the right time, Christ died for the ungodly

c. God demonstrated His LOVE for me while I was still a sinner

4) **LOVE COMES FROM GOD BECAUSE GOD IS LOVE:** *(1 John 4:10)*

a. Love covers all sins *(Proverbs 10:12)*

b. This is LOVE: not that I loved God, but that He LOVED ME

c. God showed His LOVE by sending His Son as the atoning sacrifice for sin

5) **GOD'S LOVE IS PERFECT** *(1 John 4:18)*

a. There is no fear in HIS LOVE

b. God's PERFECT LOVE drives out fear

c. Fear has to do with punishment

d. God's LOVE is perfecting me in Christ Jesus

6) **I AM LOVED BY GOD THE FATHER AND JESUS CHRIST** *(John 14:21; John 15:9)*

a. I keep myself in God's LOVE, enjoying the blessings of His Presence *(Jude 21)*

b. The gift of God is ETERNAL LIFE *(Romans 6:23b)*

7) **GOD'S LOVE IS GREATER THAN ANYTHING ELSE** *(John 15:13)*

a. And now abide faith, hope, and LOVE, these three; but the GREATEST of these IS LOVE *(1 Corinthians 13:13)*

b. LOVE NEVER FAILS *(1 Corinthians 13:8)*

c. Without LOVE . . . I AM NOTHING *(1 Corinthians 13:1–3)*

17th BOOSTER SHOT
THE JOY OF THE LORD

1) **THE JOY OF THE LORD IS MY STRENGTH** *(Nehemiah 8:10, 12,17)*

- *a.* I enjoy the blessings of the Lord
- *b.* I send portions to those who have nothing prepared
- *c.* I celebrate the goodness of God with GREAT JOY
- *d.* My GLADNESS and my JOY are very great

2) **THE LORD HAS FILLED MY HEART WITH GLADNESS AND JOY** *(Psalm 4:7)*

- *a.* I will ever sing for JOY *(Psalm 5:11)*
- *b.* Nothing in the entire world can equal the JOY of the Lord
- *c.* In God's presence is FULLNESS OF JOY *(Psalm 16:11)*

3) **MY HEART LEAPS FOR JOY BECAUSE . . .** *(Psalm 28:7; 35:27)*

- *a.* The Lord is my strength and my shield
- *b.* With my SONG I WILL PRAISE HIM
- *c.* I will shout for JOY and be GLAD
- *d.* Let the Lord be MAGNIFIED

4) **I SING FOR JOY AT THE WORKS OF THE LORD'S HANDS** *(Psalm 92:4; Psalm 95:1–2)*

- *a.* He makes me GLAD through His work
- *b.* I WILL TRIUMPH IN THE WORKS of His hands
- *c.* I will SHOUT JOYFULLY to the ROCK of my SALVATION
- *d.* I will come before His presence with THANKSGIVING, ADORATION, and PRAISE
- *e.* I will extol Him with music and song

5) **I WILL SING FOR JOY IN THE PRIVACY OF MY HOME** *(Psalm 149:5)*

  a. I have hundreds of reasons to SING AND PRAISE the LORD
  b. I will PRAISE Him wherever I go—both audibly and silently
  c. The Lord delights in me and crowns me with SALVATION *(Psalm 149:4)*

6) **EVERLASTING JOY IS THE CROWN OF MY HEAD** *(Isaiah 35:10)*

  a. I will obtain JOY and GLADNESS
  b. Sorrow and sighing shall flee away

7) **I WILL REJOICE IN THE LORD ALWAYS!** *(Philippians 3:1; Philippians 4:4)*

  a. I have been anointed with the OIL OF JOY *(Isaiah 35:10)*
  b. I consider it PURE JOY whenever I face any trial, because I KNOW the testing of my faith develops PERSEVERANCE and that finishes the work of MAKING me MATURE and COMPLETE, not lacking anything *(James 1:2–4)*
  c. I am filled with an inexpressible and glorious JOY, for I am RECEIVING the goal of my faith—the SALVATION of my SOUL *(1 Peter 1:8)*
  d. I PRAISE GOD MY SAVIOUR, who is able to keep me from falling and to present me before His GLORIOUS PRESENCE without fault and with great JOY—TO HIM GLORY, MAJESTY, POWER, and AUTHORITY through JESUS CHRIST our LORD, before all ages, now and forevermore! Amen. *(Jude 24–25)*

WHAT IS A KEY?

A KEY:

1. Provides ENTRANCE into a locked building, room, or safe, etc.
2. Represents AUTHORITY
3. Opens doors
4. Gives access to possessions
5. Opens understanding
6. Reveals mysteries
7. Symbolizes control
8. Is an aid to explanation
9. Is an aid to interpretation
10. Is a symbol of POWER
11. Is seen in "The KEYS of the KINGDOM of HEAVEN" *(Matthew 16:19)*
12. Is the POWER to bind and loose on earth and in heaven
13. Is the POWER and AUTHORITY to proclaim eternal TRUTH
14. Is seen in "The KEY of KNOWLEDGE" *(Luke 11:52)*

THE KINGDOM OF GOD IS AN ETERNAL KINGDOM

The church, the body of Christ, is God's vehicle for evangelizing the world. However, it is helpful to know and understand that the church has been corrupted and organized by man. By contrast, the kingdom of God cannot be organized, nor can it be corrupted by man. When Christ returns, the church age will end.

Jesus said clearly in Luke 17:20–21, "The kingdom of God does not come with observation . . . For indeed, *the kingdom of God is within you."*

Fundamental to New Testament truth is that the kingdom of God is a spiritual reality and dynamic to each person who receives Jesus Christ as Savior and Lord. To receive Jesus Christ as the King is to receive His kingly rule, not only in your life and *over* your affairs, but *through* your life and *by* your service and love. In Revelation 19:16, Jesus is called "KING of KINGS AND LORD OF LORDS." Who are the "kings" and the "lords" that He rules over? See Revelation 1:5–6 for the answer: "And from Jesus Christ . . . the Ruler over the *kings* of the earth . . . and has made us *kings* and *priests* to His God and Father."

In 2 Corinthians 5:20, we believers are called "ambassadors for Christ." An ambassador is a representative of a kingdom, or government, in a foreign country. We as God's children represent the KINGDOM OF GOD on this earth. An ambassador does not have personal opinions when he deals with people of the nation he is appointed to. Likewise, we as believers should also speak for our King, who is Jesus. Our constitution is the Word of God.

18th BOOSTER SHOT
KEYS OF THE KINGDOM

These are not keys *to* the kingdom. There is only one key *to* the kingdom: that is to "be born again" (John 3:3, 5). These are keys for believers *in* the kingdom.

1) **THE WORD OF GOD** *(Deuteronomy 8:3b and Isaiah 40:8)*

- a. The Word of God is living and active *(Hebrews 4:12)*
- *b.* With the WORD I defeat the enemy *(Matthew 4:1–11)*
- *c.* By the WORD I have power over sin *(Psalm 119:11)*
- *d.* In the WORD I walk in HEALTH *(Psalm 107:20)*
- *e.* With the WORD I bring HEALING to others *(Mark 16:18)*
- *f.* Through the WORD I am washed clean *(John 15:3; Ephesians 5:26)*

2) **THE BLOOD OF JESUS** *(Hebrews 9: 16--22)*

- *a.* It washes and keeps me clean *(1 John 1:7)*
- *b.* It brings me near to God *(Ephesians 2:13)*
- *c.* By His Blood, I overcome the adversary *(Revelation 12:11)*
- *d.* It protects me from death *(Exodus 12:13)*
- *e.* It takes away ALL MY SIN *(John 1:29)*

3) **THE NAME OF JESUS** *(Philippians 2:9–10)*

- *a.* HE WILL DO whatever I ask in His NAME *(John 14:12–14)*
- *b.* My SALVATION is in His NAME *(Acts 4:12)*
- *c.* My HEALING is in His NAME *(Acts 3:1–16)*
- *d.* I have ABUNDANT LIFE in His NAME *(John 10:10)*
- *e.* I have VICTORY in His NAME *(Philippians 2:9–11)*

4) **THE PRAYER OF FAITH AND AGREEMENT** *(Matthew 18: 19–20)*

a. I RECEIVE according to my FAITH *(Matthew 9:28–30)*
b. I RENOUNCE DOUBT and ASK in FAITH *(Mark 11:22–24)*
c. I SEEK AGREEMENT to BOOST my FAITH *(Matthew 18:19–20)*
d. The PRAYER of FAITH HEALS the sick *(James 5:13–16)*
e. God's ears are open to my prayers *(I Peter 3:12)*

5) **PRAISE, WORSHIP, AND SONG** *(Psalm 22:3; Psalm 33:3; Deuteronomy 10:21; John 9:31*

a. The Lord is PRESENT when I PRAISE Him *(Psalm 22:3)*
b. I SING praises to His Name to WIN the battle *(Acts 16:25–26)*
c. I WORSHIP the Lord in Spirit and in Truth *(John 4:23–24)*
d. PRAISE and the WORD are my weapons of warfare *(Psalm 149:1–6)*
e. My warfare is in the spiritual realm *(2 Corinthians 10:3–5)*

6) **TESTIMONY AND CONFESSION OF FAITH** *(Hebrews 4:14; Luke 21:13)*

a. I have ETERNAL LIFE in the SON of GOD *(1 John 5:10–13)*
b. By the word of my TESTIMONY, I overcome the devil *(Revelation 12:11)*
c. I am not ashamed of the GOSPEL of JESUS CHRIST *(Romans 1:16)*

7) **TITHING AND GIVING** *(Malachi 3:8–12)*

a. I GIVE and it is GIVEN TO ME *(Luke 6:38)*
b. I SOW generously and I REAP generously *(2 Corinthians 9:6)*
c. I GIVE CHEERFULLY, and God's GRACE ABOUNDS *(2 Corinthians 9:7–8)*
d. God supplies ALL my needs according to His glorious riches in Christ Jesus *(Philippians 4:19)*
e. I GIVE a tenth (a tithe) of my income, and God pours out BLESSINGS *(Malachi 3:8–11)*

19th BOOSTER SHOT

THE REDEEMING BLOOD OF JESUS CHRIST

1) **THE BLOOD OF CHRIST IS THE BLOOD OF THE NEW COVENANT** *(Matthew 26:28)*
    a. His BLOOD was shed for the FORGIVENESS of my sins
    b. Without the shedding of blood there is no remission of sins *(Hebrews 9:20–22)*

2) **THROUGH FAITH IN THE BLOOD OF CHRIST I AM JUSTIFIED** *(Romans 5:9)*
    a. By His BLOOD I am saved from the wrath of God toward sin
    b. The BLOOD that was applied by faith has cleansed me from sin
    c. Being justified, I stand before God in the righteousness of Christ

3) **THROUGH FAITH IN THE BLOOD OF CHRIST I HAVE BEEN REDEEMED** *(Romans 3:24)*
    a. Christ PAID the RANSOM for my deliverance from sin
    b. I have been set free from the evil and penalty of sin
    c. I am REDEEMED and FORGIVEN according to the riches of His GRACE *(Ephesians 1:7)*
    d. The BLOOD of Christ has brought me intimately near to God *(Ephesians 2:13)*
    e. Through the BLOOD shed on the CROSS, Christ has made PEACE for me by bringing me into HARMONY with God as my Father *(Colossians 1:20)*

4) **THE BLOOD OF CHRIST CLEANSES MY CONSCIENCE** *(Hebrews 9:14)*
   a. My conscience has been cleansed from dead rituals and dead works
   b. I have been made fit to SERVE THE LIVING GOD
   c. I strive to have a conscience without offense toward God and men *(Acts 24:16)*

5) **THE BLOOD OF JESUS CHRIST PURIFIES ME FROM ALL SIN** *(1 John 1:7)*
   a. Walking in the LIGHT of Christ, we have FELLOWSHIP with one another
   b. Confession of sin brings FORGIVENESS and CLEANSING (1 John 1:9)
   c. If I commit sin as a child of God, I have an ADVOCATE with the Father, Jesus Christ the Righteous (1 John 2:1)

6) **BY THE BLOOD OF THE LAMB—JESUS CHRIST—I OVERCOME SATAN, MY ACCUSER** *(Revelation 2:11)*
   a. Satan was cast out of heaven to earth. He is a "blackmailer" through guilt and accusations. His main target is the citizens of the kingdom of God.
   b. The BLOOD of the Lamb has satisfied all of the charges against me
   c. With His BLOOD I was purchased for God (1 Peter 1:17–19)
   d. God has provided me with every necessary provision to DEFEAT SATAN
   e. God has declared that I am RIGHTEOUS and VICTORIOUS through the BLOOD

7) **THE BLOOD OF CHRIST PURCHASED THE GIFT OF ETERNAL LIFE FOR ME** *(John 6:53–63)*

a. By partaking in the covenant BLOOD of Christ, I am joined to God and receive the benefits of HIS LIFE

b. His flesh and BLOOD point to His crucifixion and Himself as the ONLY SOURCE of ETERNAL LIFE

c. HE IS THE BREAD OF LIFE, and I partake of Him

d. The words that He speaks are SPIRIT, AND THEY ARE LIFE

e. I RECEIVE His Word

20th BOOSTER SHOT
POWER POINTS IN GOD'S WORD

1) **THE POWER OF GOD'S WORD** *(Hebrews 4:12)*

a. The Word of God is LIVING and POWERFUL
b. It is SHARPER than a TWO-EDGED SWORD
c. It has the POWER to DIVIDE soul and spirit
d. The Word reveals that which is spiritual and that which is soulish
e. What marrow is to the bones, The Word is to MY LIFE
f. The Word discerns the thoughts and intents of my heart

2) **JESUS IS THE LIVING WORD** *(John 1:14)*

a. The WORD became FLESH and DWELT among us
b. His GLORY was manifested on earth—His SPLENDOR, RADIANCE, and MAJESTY
c. His GLORY—of the FATHER—is full of GRACE and TRUTH

3) **THE POWER IN THE NAME OF JESUS** *(Philippians 2:9–11)*

a. His Name is A NAME above every name
b. His Name is exalted to the HIGHEST POSITION
c. EVERY KNEE WILL BOW in heaven, on the earth, and under the earth
d. EVERY TONGUE WILL CONFESS that Jesus Christ is LORD to the glory of God the FATHER
e. No other name can save us *(Acts 4:12)*
f. I have HEALING in the Name of JESUS *(Acts 3:16)*
g. In the NAME of JESUS we cast out demons *(Mark 16:17)*
h. We PRAY in the Name of JESUS
i. WE ASK in the Name of JESUS *(John 14:12–14)*

4) **THE POWER IN THE BLOOD OF JESUS**

a. The Lord Jesus purchased the church for God with HIS OWN BLOOD *(Acts 20:28)*

b. I am REDEEMED by the BLOOD of Jesus Christ *(Romans 3:24–25)*

c. It is the SHED BLOOD of Christ that satisfied the requirements of God's justice *(Romans 3:25–26)*

d. I have been JUSTIFIED by HIS BLOOD *(Romans 5:9)*

e. I have been brought into RIGHT RELATIONSHIP with GOD

f. The Son of God made PEACE through the BLOOD of the CROSS (Colossians 1:20)

g. The BLOOD of CHRIST CLEANSES my conscience from dead works to SERVE GOD

h. I OVERCOME Satan by the BLOOD of the LAMB and my TESTIMONY

5) **THE POWER OF THE HOLY SPIRIT** *(Acts 1:8)*

a. I shall receive POWER when the HOLY SPIRIT has come upon me

b. I receive POWER to be a WITNESS for CHRIST by the HOLY SPIRIT

c. I ABOUND in HOPE by the POWER of the HOLY SPIRIT *(Romans 15:13)*

d. My body is the temple of the HOLY SPIRIT who is in me from God *(1 Corinthians 6:19)*

e. The POWER of the gospel is in the WORD and POWER is in the HOLY SPIRIT *(1 Thessalonians 1:5)*

f. God's MERCY SAVED me through the WASHING of REGENERATION and the RENEWING of the HOLY SPIRIT *(Titus 3:5)*

21st BOOSTER SHOT
A THANKFUL HEART

1) **LET US COME BEFORE HIS PRESENCE WITH THANKSGIVING** *(Psalm 95:2)*
   - *a.* I WILL SHOUT joyfully to the LORD with psalms
   - *b.* I WILL LIFT my hands in praise and THANKSGIVING
   - *c.* I WILL WORSHIP and bow down (Psalm 95:6)

2) **I WILL THANK AND PRAISE HIM MORNING, NOON, AND EVENING** *(1 Chronicles 23:30)*
   - *a.* I WILL GIVE THANKS to God among unbelievers (Psalm 18:49)
   - *b.* I WILL GIVE THANKS at the remembrance of His NAME (Psalm 30:4)
   - *c.* I WILL GIVE THANKS to the Lord, for HE IS GOOD (Psalm 107:1)
   - *d.* His MERCY endures forever

3) **THANKS BE TO GOD, WHO GIVES US THE VICTORY THROUGH OUR LORD JESUS CHRIST** *(1 Corinthians 15:57)*
   - *a.* THANKS be to GOD who ALWAYS leads us in TRIUMPH IN CHRIST *(2 Corinthians 2:14)*
   - *b.* THANKS be to God for His INDESCRIBABLE GIFT! *(2 Corinthians 9:15)*
   - *c.* I GIVE THANKS for the exceeding GRACE OF GOD in me *(2 Corinthians 9:14)*

4) **I GIVE THANKS ALWAYS FOR ALL THINGS TO GOD THE FATHER** *(Ephesians 5:20)*

a. I give THANKS to the Father, who has qualified me to be a PARTAKER of the INHERITANCE of the saints IN THE LIGHT *(Colossians 1:12)*

b. He has DELIVERED me from the power of darkness

c. He has TRANSFERRED me into the KINGDOM of the SON OF HIS LOVE

5) **WHATEVER I DO, IN WORD OR DEED…I GIVE THANKS TO GOD THE FATHER THROUGH OUR LORD JESUS CHRIST:** *(Colossians 3:17)*

a. I GIVE THANKS in everything, for this is the WILL OF GOD *(I Thessalonians 5:18)*

b. I offer the SACRIFICE of PRAISE to God: the fruit of my lips *(Hebrews 13:15)*

c. I GIVE THANKS TO HIS NAME

6) **I WILL PROCLAIM THE WONDROUS WORKS OF GOD WITH THE VOICE OF THANKSGIVING** *(Psalm 26:7)*

a. I will offer to God THANKSGIVING *(Psalm 50:14)*

b. I will pay my vows to the MOST HIGH *(Psalm 50:14)*

c. He WILL DELIVER me in the day of trouble *(Psalm 50:15)*

d. I WILL GLORIFY THE LORD with a testimony of THANKSGIVING

7) **I WILL PRAY IN FAITH WITH THANKSGIVING** *(Philippians 4:6)*

a. I will make my requests known to God in faith . . .

b. And the PEACE of GOD will guard my heart and mind *(Philippians 4:7)*

c. The elders fell on their faces before the THRONE and WORSHIPED GOD, saying, "AMEN! Blessing and glory and wisdom, THANKSGIVING and honor and power and MIGHT, be to our GOD FOREVER and EVER. AMEN." *(Revelation 7:11–12)*

22nd BOOSTER SHOT

WALKING, TALKING, LIVING IN THE SPIRIT

1) **I WILL NOT WALK ACCORDING TO THE FLESH** *(Romans 8:1, 4)*

- *a.* There is no condemnation on me; I AM IN CHRIST *(Romans 8:1)*
- *b.* I live according to the LAW of the SPIRIT of LIFE in Christ JESUS *(Romans 8:2)*
- *c.* I AM FREE from the law of sin and death
- *d.* I've been liberated, acquitted, delivered from the dominion of sin

2) **I WILL LIVE MY LIFE ACCORDING TO THE SPIRIT** *(Romans 8:5)*

- *a.* I WILL NOT set my mind on things of the flesh
- *b.* I WIL set my mind on things of the SPIRIT
- *c.* If I choose to be carnally minded, I walk in DEATH *(Romans 8:6)*
- *d.* If I CHOOSE to be SPIRITUALLY MINDED, I walk in LIFE and PEACE
- *e.* The carnal mind is at enmity with God and cannot please God *(Romans 8:9–11)*

3) **AS A BELIEVER, I AM NOT IN THE FLESH BUT IN THE SPIRIT** *(Romans 8:9–11)*

- *a.* My body is dead BECAUSE OF SIN
- *b.* My SPIRIT IS ALIVE because of the righteousness of CHRIST
- *c.* The Spirit that raised Christ from the dead DWELLS IN ME
- *d.* The same SPIRIT will give life to my mortal body to OBEY God's WORD

e. As I walk in the SPIRIT and FEED on God's Word, I WILL GROW STRONG

4) **I AM NOT A DEBTOR TO THE FLESH; I DON'T OWE THE FLESH ANYTHING!** *(Romans 8:12–14)*

a. If I walk according to the flesh, I WILL DIE

b. The Holy Spirit gives me POWER to put to death the works of the flesh

c. I am a CHILD OF GOD because I am led by the SPIRIT OF GOD

5) **GOD PROVIDES HEALING AND PROVISION FOR THE BODY, BUT HE DOES NOT CATER TO WHIMS AND FRIVOLITIES OF THE FLESHLY MIND** *(James 4:1–3; 5:15)*

a. I SET MY MIND on THINGS ABOVE, not on things of the earth *(Colossians 3:2)*

b. I have been raised (made spiritually ALIVE) with Christ *(Colossians 3:1)*

c. Christ is seated at the RIGHT HAND OF GOD

d. I reckon myself to be DEAD INDEED TO SIN *(Romans 6:11)*

e. I AM ALIVE TO GOD in Christ Jesus my LORD

f. I DO NOT let sin reign in my mortal body *(Romans 6:12)*

6) **IF I WALK IN THE SPIRIT, I WILL NOT FULFILL THE LUSTS OF THE FLESH** *(Galatians 5:16)*

a. I declare WAR AGAINST THE LUSTS of the FLESH *(Galatians 5:17)*

b. In ALL THESE THINGS I am MORE THAN A CONQUEROR *(Romans 8:37)*

c. The Holy Spirit WILL HELP ME in my weakness *(Romans 8:26)*

7) **LIVING IN THE SPIRIT, I WALK IN FORGIVENESS TOWARDS OTHERS** *(Colossians 3:12–13)*

a. I will show TENDER MERCIES and KINDNESS to others

b. I will walk in HUMILITY, MEEKNESS, and LONGSUFFERING

c. I RELEASE ALL offenses and refuse to enact any penalty due another

d. I REFUSE to allow any offense to affect my relationships

e. TO FORGIVE IS A CONSCIOUS CHOICE I MAKE —IT SETS ME FREE

23rd BOOSTER SHOT

LIVING WITH AN AWARENESS OF THE PRESENCE OF GOD

One of the saddest events in the history of mankind is found in Genesis 3:8–4:16. Adam and Eve "hid themselves from the presence of God among the trees of the garden." They thought they were hiding, when God knew exactly where they were—hiding among the very things that God had created for their benefit and enjoyment. We know the reason: disobedience. Today, through the blood of Christ, we can come back into the presence of God.

1) **THERE IS PEACE AND REST IN THE PRESENCE OF THE LORD** *(Exodus 33:14)*
   - *a.* I am SECURE in the PRESENCE OF THE LORD
   - *b.* I DWELL PEACEFULLY in the PRESENCE OF THE LORD
   - *c.* The world will be silenced in the PRESENCE OF THE LORD *(Zephaniah 1:7)*

2) **THERE IS FULLNESS OF JOY IN THE PRESENCE OF THE LORD** *(Psalm 16:11)*
   - *a.* I WALK in the PATH OF LIFE in His presence
   - *b.* At His right hand I find spiritual PLEASURES FOREVERMORE
   - *c.* I discover a life-changing DEVOTION to God in His PRESENCE
   - *d.* In God's PRESENCE I find wisdom and protection from the enemy *(Psalm 17:2–9)*

3) **I WILL FOLLOW THE EXAMPLE OF DAVID TO LOVE THE BLESSINGS OF GOD'S PRESENCE** *(Psalm 21:1–7)*

a. YOU have made me exceedingly GLAD WITH YOUR PRESENCE
b. I have JOY in the Lord's STRENGTH
c. I REJOICE GREATLY in the SALVATION of the LORD
d. HE fulfills my heart's desire
e. The LORD will MEET ME with BLESSINGS of GOODNESS
f. The LORD will prolong my life to its fullest extent
g. In HIS PRESENCE I will not be moved

4) **I AM SAFE AND SECURE IN THE SECRET PLACE OF YOUR PRESENCE** *(Psalm 31:19–20)*

a. IN YOUR PRESENCE, Your GOODNESS is GREAT
b. I WILL manifest Your presence wherever I go
c. You, LORD, will protect me from the evil plots of man
d. YOU will keep me from the strife of tongues

5) **JESUS SAID, "SURELY I AM WITH YOU ALWAYS, EVEN TO THE END OF THE AGE"** *(Matthew 28:20)*

a. JESUS will NEVER LEAVE ME NOR FORSAKE ME *(Hebrew 13:5; Deuteronomy 31:6)*
b. JESUS DWELLS IN ME by His SPIRIT, He is with me FOREVER *(John 14:16)*
c. When I meet with other believers, JESUS is there in our midst *(Matthew 18:20)*
d. Christ IN ME the HOPE OF GLORY *(Colossians 1:27)*
e. CHRIST WITH ME A GLORIOUS STORY

24th BOOSTER SHOT
WALKING IN WISDOM

1) **THE FEAR (RESPECT, REVERENCE, AWE) OF THE LORD IS THE BEGINNING OF KNOWLEDGE** *(Proverbs 1:7)*

a. In HUMILITY I prepare my heart and mind to RECEIVE WISDOM and INSTRUCTION

b. The LORD gives WISDOM; I will ask and receive *(Proverbs 2:6; James 1:5)*

c. I open my heart to receive WISDOM; KNOWLEDGE is pleasant to my soul (Proverbs 2:10)

d. I will trust in the Lord with all my heart *(Proverbs 3:5–6)*

e. I will not depend on my own carnal mind for true understanding

f. I will acknowledge the LORD in all my ways

g. AND HE WILL DIRECT MY LIFE

2) **I WILL HONOR THE LORD WITH ALL MY TALENTS, GIFTS, AND POSSESSIONS** *(Proverbs 3:9)*

a. I will give proportionately of all my increase

b. As a result, my bank account will be filled with plenty

c. My heart will overflow with the JOY of the LORD *(Nehemiah 8:10)*

3) **I WILL SEARCH FOR WISDOM AND UNDERSTANDING, AND I WILL FIND HER** *(Matthew 7:7)*

a. Wisdom is the PRINCIPAL THING *(Proverbs 4:7)*

b. When I walk in WISDOM, my steps will not be hindered *(Proverbs 4:12)*
c. When I run I will not stumble *(Proverbs 4:12)*
d. I WILL take FIRM HOLD of the Lord's INSTRUCTION *(Proverbs 4:13)*
e. I WILL NOT despise the CORRECTION OF the Lord *(Proverbs 3:11)*

4) **THE WISDOM OF THE LORD IS ETERNAL** *(Proverbs 8:22–31)*

a. With WISDOM I am able to govern and discipline myself by use of reason *(Proverbs 8:12)*
b. I FEAR the LORD, and I HATE EVIL *(Proverbs 8:13)*
c. Pride and arrogance have no part of my life
d. I WILL NOT speak perversely (improperly, corruptly, in a way opposed to God)
e. In finding WISDOM, I find LIFE and obtain favor from the Lord (Proverbs 8:35)

5) **THE FEAR OF THE LORD IS THE BEGINNING OF WISDOM** *(Proverbs 9:10)*

a. By WISDOM my days will be multiplied *(Proverbs 9:11)*
b. By WISDOM, years of life will be added to me
c. When I walk with integrity, I WALK SECURELY (*Proverbs 10:9)*
d. When my mouth SPEAKS RIGHTEOUSLY, it is a WELL OF LIFE *(Proverbs 10:11)*
e. The actions of the wicked nullify the words of their mouth *(Psalm 55:21)*
f. A WISE person stores up knowledge *(Proverbs 10:14)*

g. The BLESSING of the Lord makes me rich without sorrow *(Proverbs 10:22)*

6) **I WILL WALK IN THE WISDOM OF RIGHTEOUSNESS** *(Proverbs 12:3–14)*
   a. The ROOT of the RIGHTEOUS cannot be moved *(Proverbs 12:3)*
   b. The HOUSE of the RIGHTEOUS WILL STAND *(Proverbs 12:7)*
   c. The ROOT of the RIGHTEOUS yields FRUIT *(Proverbs 12:12)*
   d. RIGHTEOUSNESS exalts a nation *(Proverbs 14:34)*

7) **THE TONGUE OF THE WISE USES KNOWLEDGE RIGHTLY** *(Proverbs 15:2)*
   a. A wholesome (healing) tongue is a TREE OF LIFE *(Proverbs 15:4)*
   b. The lips of the WISE spread KNOWLEDGE *(Proverbs 15:7)*
   c. Death and LIFE are in the power of the tongue *(Proverbs 18:20)*

25th BOOSTER SHOT

THE BLESSINGS OF WALKING IN THE FEAR OF THE LORD

1) **THE FEAR OF THE LORD IS CLEAN, ENDURING FOREVER** *(Psalm 19:9)*

- *a.* It can be learned *(Psalm 34:11)*
- *b.* It is the beginning of WISDOM *(Psalm 111:10)*
- *c.* It is the beginning of KNOWLEDGE *(Proverbs 1:7)*
- *d.* It is the way of BLESSINGS *(Psalm 112:1)*

2) **THE PROMISES OF FEARING THE LORD** *(Psalm 25:12–15)*

- *a.* Guidance: "him shall HE teach in the way HE chooses"
- *b.* Prosperity: "he himself shall dwell in PROSPERITY"
- *c.* Posterity: "his descendants shall inherit the earth"
- *d.* Divine confidence: "the secret of the Lord is with those who FEAR HIM"
- *e.* Covenant: "He will show them HIS COVENANT"
- *f.* Deliverance: "HE shall pluck my feet out of the net"

3) **THE FEAR OF THE LORD IS NOT BEING AFRAID** *(Psalm 27:1–6)*

- *a.* The fear of God is not a terror that He is against us or will strike without cause or warning. Rather the FEAR OF THE LORD produces WISE, HEALTHY ACTIONS *(Exodus 1:17)*
- *b.* Whom shall I fear? *(Psalm 27:1a)*
- *c.* Of whom shall I be afraid? *(Psalm 27:1b)*
- *d.* My heart SHALL NOT FEAR *(Psalm 27:3)*

e. For in the time of trouble He shall HIDE ME IN HIS PAVILION; In the SECRET place of His TABERNACLE He shall HIDE ME *(Psalm 27:5)*

4) **THE FEAR OF THE LORD BRINGS HEALING** *(Malachi 4:2)*

a. The Son of Righteousness shall arise with HEALING in His wings

b. HEALING: a restoration of HEALTH, remedy, cure, medicine, tranquility, deliverance, refreshing

c. Salvation is God's rescue of the entire person, and HEALING is His complete repair of that person

d. HEAL my soul, for I have sinned against You *(Psalm 41:4)*

e. He HEALS the brokenhearted and binds up their wounds *(Psalm 147:3)*

5) **IN THE FEAR OF THE LORD IS A PLACE OF REFUGE** *(Proverbs 14:26)*

a. A shelter of PROTECTION

b. A fortress for SECURITY and CONFIDENCE

c. A place of TRUST and HOPE

6) **THE FEAR OF THE LORD IS A FOUNTAIN OF LIFE** *(Proverbs 14:27)*

a. The fountain of LIFE refreshes the WHOLE OF LIFE

b. Jesus said He would give a FOUNTAIN OF WATER springing up into EVERLASTING LIFE *(John 4:14)*

7) **THE FEAR OF THE LORD LEADS TO ABUNDANT LIFE** *(John 10:10; Proverbs 19:23)*

a. "I have come that they may have LIFE more ABUNDANTLY"

b. "He who believes in ME . . . out of his heart will flow RIVERS of LIVING WATER" *(John 7:38)*

26th BOOSTER SHOT
WORSHIPING GOD IN SPIRIT AND IN TRUTH

1) **I MUST WORSHIP GOD IN SPIRIT AND TRUTH** *(John 4:22–24)*

a. I am convinced in my mind and spirit that I WORSHIP THE ONLY TRUE GOD

b. I KNOW the only true God has given me SALVATION

c. I WORSHIP God as my heavenly Father, Creator of all things

d. I submit to the Holy Spirit in WORSHIP

e. I KNOW God's Son, Jesus Christ, is the WAY, the TRUTH, and the LIFE *(John 14:6)*

2) **I WORSHIP THE GOD OF ABRAHAM, ISAAC, AND JACOB** *(Acts 3:13)*

a. When Leah bore her last son with Jacob, she said, "NOW I WILL PRAISE THE LORD." She called him "JUDAH" which means PRAISE *(Genesis 29:35).*

b. When Jacob pronounced a prophecy and blessing over his sons, he gives JUDAH the highest blessing *(Genesis 49:8–12)*

c. In David's SONG OF THANKSGIVING *(1 Chronicles 16:7–36),* he reminds us of the PROMISES God made to Abraham, Isaac, and Jacob *(1 Chronicles 16:14–22)*

3) **THREE LEVELS OF WORSHIP: BODY WORSHIP, SOUL WORSHIP, AND WORSHIP IN THE SPIRIT** *(Matthew 15:8—-9; 2 Timothy 3:5; John 4:23–24)*
    a. BODY: Imitate, go with the flow, physical motions, sing the song
    b. SOUL: Have to "feel" it before I can enter in
    c. SPIRIT: True worship in the spirit is a constant attitude for the believer
        i. Sitting quietly in worship
        ii. Rejoicing audibly in praises (words or songs) *(1 Corinthians 14:15)*
        iii. Worship in the spirit brings the soul and body under submission
        iv. David speaks to his soul to encourage himself *(Psalm 42:5,11: "Hope in God"; "HELP is on the way"; "my countenance is lifted")*

4) **CORPORATE WORSHIP: THE GATHERING TOGETHER** *(Numbers 21:16–17)*
    a. God's INSTRUCTION: "Gather the people together"
    b. God's PROMISE: "I will give them water" (life)
    c. People's RESPONSIBILITY: SING—"Spring up, O well! *All* of you sing to it"
    d. Our LESSON: In times of pressure, anxiety, or depression, do not stay alone. Gather with God's people, the PRAISING PEOPLE
    e. Regardless of your personal feelings, join in audible PRAISE and sing to YOUR WELL the Living God, the FOUNTAIN, that flows from deep within
    f. Let your SONG be one of THANKSGIVING for past blessings and a SONG of FAITH in God's PROMISES for the present and the future!

5) **WORSHIPING "WITH ONE ACCORD" BRINGS THE PRESENCE AND POWER OF THE HOLY SPIRIT** *(Acts 1:14 and Acts 2:1–4)*

   a. "With one accord": Being unanimous, having mutual consent, being in agreement, having group unity, having one mind and purpose . . . a harmony leading to action. *(Acts 2:1, Matthew 18:19–20)*

   b. The result of gathering with one accord: "And SUDDENLY there came a SOUND from heaven" *(Acts 2:2)*

   c. Cleansed by the BLOOD of Jesus, we have boldness to enter in to the HOLIEST PLACE, a new and living way which He opened up for us *(Hebrews 10:19–25)*

   d. Do not forsake the assembling of ourselves *(Hebrews 10:25)*

27th BOOSTER SHOT
HOW TO BOOST YOUR PRAYER LIFE

1) **ALWAYS PRAY IN AN HONEST AND SINCERE MANNER** *(Matthew 6:5–8)*

  a. When you pray, don't pray like a hypocrite-pretender—*prayers designed for the ears of men, not God*
  b. Experience times of private prayer often and regularly
  c. Pray to the Father who will meet you in the secret place
  d. Jesus said, "the Father will reward you openly"
  e. Prayers in FAITH do not use vain repetitions; the Father knows what we need before we even ask Him

2) **GOD'S WORD INSTRUCTS ME TO COME BOLDLY WHEN I PRAY** *(Hebrews 4:16)*

  a. I can speak to God without reservation, with frankness, with full and open speech
  b. We approach the THRONE OF GRACE, not of judgment
  c. We obtain MERCY for the past and GRACE for the present and future

3) **WRESTLING WITH GOD: THE EXAMPLE OF JACOB** *(Genesis 32:22-32)*

  a. I must be willing to isolate myself from others for a personal encounter with God
  b. I must be willing to stay as long as it takes for the answer
  c. Hosea sees Jacob as a model to be emulated whenever I face a difficulty or have a need for a character transformation *(Hosea 12:2–6)*

d. Hosea admonishes us to WAIT on our God CONTINUALLY *(Hosea 12:6b)*

4) **THE LORD IS GOOD TO THOSE WHO WAIT FOR HIM** *(Lamentations 3:25)*

a. I will wait with expectation and hope, because the LORD is my portion *(Lamentations 3:24)*

b. It is good to hope and wait quietly for the answer *(Lamentations 3:26)*

c. There is a special blessing that comes in the waiting *(Isaiah 40:31)*

d. My strength is RENEWED like the eagle *(Isaiah 40:31)*

5) **HOW TO PRAY WITHOUT CEASING** *(1 Thessalonians 5:17)*

a. I must live with an awareness of the PRESENCE of GOD

b. Wherever I am; whatever I am doing; HE IS WITH ME by His Spirit

c. Prayer is a constant ATTITUDE of enjoying continual COMMUNION with the Lord

d. I must be READY to PRAY in season or out of season whenever the need arises

e. My first spiritual instinct in any decision making should be to pray

6) **GOD IS A PRAYER-ANSWERING GOD** *(Matthew 21:22)*

a. God answers when I BELIEVE for what I am praying

b. I must cast out doubt before I ask God in prayer *(James 1:5–8) c.* Jesus gives us a formula for SUCCESS in Matthew 7:7: ASK . . . SEEK . . . KNOCK. The answer: GIVEN . . . FOUND . . . OPENED

7) **PRAYING WITH THANKSGIVING WITHOUT BEING ANXIOUS** *(Philippians 4:6)*

a. SUPPLICATION: Focusing with intensity in extended prayer and fully transferring the burden or request into God's hands

b. A prayer in faith will not take back what has been given to God

c. The prayer of FAITH will bring the PEACE of God that will guard my heart from nagging anxiety

SPIRITUAL PRESCRIPTION'S FOR THE BELIEVER

SPIRITUAL PRESCRIPTION'S FOR THE BELIEVER

TEN COMMANDMENTS OF SUCCESS

1. Don't allow the enemy to distract you
2. Rebuke any form of discouragement
3. Don't listen to the critics and naysayers
4. Do not indulge in gossip
5. Speak the Word of Faith
6. Don't become critical
7. Encourage and edify others
8. Promote truth and righteousness
9. Remember, your life, your attitude, and your conversation are a witness to those with whom you come in contact
10. In ALL things you do, determine to excel to the best of your God-given abilities

****

TEN CONFESSIONS OF SUCCESS

1. I will not allow the enemy to distract me
2. I will reject any form of discouragement
3. I will not listen to a critical spirit
4. I will not indulge in any form of gossip
5. I will speak the Word of Faith
6. I will be positive and thankful
7. I will encourage others
8. I will promote truth and righteousness
9. I will remember that my life is a witness to others

10. I am determined to excel to the best of my God-given abilities in everything I do

****

GROWING STRONG IN FAITH

What I must KNOW and BELIEVE as a born-again Christian:

- I am a NEW CREATION IN CHRIST *(2 Corinthians 5:17; 1 Peter 1:23)*
- The kingdom of God is WITHIN ME *(Luke 17:21)*
- I have an ANOINTING from God by the Holy Spirit *(1 John 2:20–27)*
- God Himself, by His Spirit, dwells and abides in me *(John 14:16–18; Romans 8:11)*
- God will never leave me or forsake me *(Matthew 28:20; Hebrews 13:5)*
- God says I CAN do all things through Christ who STRENGTHENS me *(Philippians 4:13)*
- God says I am MORE than a CONQUEROR through Christ *(Romans 8:37)*

WHO AM I IN CHRIST?

"But we all, with unveiled face, beholding as in a mirror the glory of the Lord, are being transformed into the same image from glory to glory, just as by the Spirit of the Lord." (2 Corinthians 3:18)

1. I am God's child *(John 1:12)*
2. I am born again of the imperishable seed of the Word of God which lives and endures forever *(1 Peter 1:23)*
3. I am God's workmanship, created in Christ Jesus to do good works *(Ephesians 2:10)*
4. I am a new creation in Christ *(2 Corinthians 5:17)*
5. I am born of the Spirit, alive to God *(Hebrews 12:23; 1 Thessalonians 5:23)*
6. I am a believer, and the light of the gospel shines in my mind *(2 Corinthians 4:4)*
7. I am an heir of God and a joint-heir with Christ *(Romans 8:17)*
8. I am more than a conqueror through Christ who loves me *(Romans 8:37)*
9. I am an overcomer by the blood of the Lamb and the word of my testimony *(Revelation 12:11)*
10. I am a partaker of God's divine nature *(2 Peter 1:4)*
11. I am an ambassador for Christ *(2 Corinthians 5:20)*
12. I am part of a chosen people, a royal priesthood, and a holy nation *(1 Peter 2:9)*
13. I am the righteousness of God in Jesus Christ *(2 Corinthians 5:21)*
14. I am a temple of the Holy Spirit; I am not my own *(1 Corinthians 6:19)*
15. I am a light in the world *(Matthew 5:14)*
16. I am forgiven of all my sins and washed in His blood *(Ephesians 1:7)*

17. I am one of God's chosen people, holy and dearly loved. I am clothed with compassion, kindness, humility, gentleness, and patience. *(Colossians 3:12)*
18. I am delivered from the power of darkness and translated into God's kingdom of light and love *(Colossians 1:12–13)*
19. I am redeemed from the curse of sin, sickness, and poverty *(Galatians 3:13; Deuteronomy 28:15–68)*
20. I am firmly rooted, built up, and strengthened in my faith *(Colossians 2:7)*
21. I am greatly loved by God *(Ephesians 2:4; 1 Thessalonians 1:4; 1 John 3:1)*
22. I am alive in Christ in me *(Ephesians 2:5)*
23. I am born of God; I do not continue in sin. I am safe in God, and the evil one cannot harm me. *(1 John 5:18)*

THINGS I HAVE IN CHRIST
and
THINGS I CAN DO THROUGH CHRIST

- I have the mind of Christ *(1 Corinthians 2:16; Philippians 2:5)*
- I have the peace of God which transcends all understanding *(Philippians 4:7)*
- I have the Greater One living in me *(1 John 4:4)*
- I have received the gift of righteousness, and I reign in this life through Jesus Christ *(Romans 5:17)*
- I have received the Spirit of Wisdom and Revelation; the eyes of my understanding are being enlightened *(Ephesians 1:17–18)*
- I have received the power of the Holy Spirit *(Acts 1:8)*
- Because I am a believer:
    - I have power to lay hands on the sick and see them recover
    - I have ability to speak in new tongues
    - I have authority to cast out demons
    - I have authority over all the power of the enemy *(Mark 16:17; Luke 10:19)*
- I have taken off my old self with its practices and put on the new self, which is being renewed in knowledge in the image of its Creator *(Colossians 3:10)*
- I have no lack, the Lord is my Shepherd *(Psalm 23:1)*
- God supplies all my needs according to His glorious riches in Christ Jesus *(Philippians 4:19)*
- I can do all things through Christ who gives me strength *(Philippians 4:13)*
- I can extinguish all the flaming arrows of Satan with the shield of faith *(Ephesians 6:16)*

- I declare the praises of God, because He called me out of darkness into His marvelous light *(1 Peter 2:9)*
- I walk in the light of Jesus Christ *(1 John 1:7)*
- I have fellowship with Father God and His Son, Jesus Christ *(1 John 1:3)*
- I have an anointing from the Holy One who leads me in truth *(1 John 1:20)*
- I give a tithe (10%) of my earnings to the house of the Lord and offerings to missions and other ministries as the Holy Spirit leads me *(Malachi 3:10)*

LIVING A VICTORIOUS CHRISTIAN LIFE

1) **LOOKING TO JESUS: The Living Word…….John 14:6**
   - Jesus is THE WAY, the TRUTH, and the LIFE

2) **LIVING BY FAITH: In The Cross of Christ……..Romans 6:1-14**
   - When you have died to sin, you no longer live in sin
   - Baptized into Christ, "baptized into His death" – ON THE CROSS
   - Buried with Him, raised with Him, "Walk in newness of life"
   - Our old man was crucified with Him, no longer slaves to sin
   - "For he who has died has been freed from sin" *(v.7)*
   - "If we died with Christ, we believe that we shall also live with Him" – NOW!
   - The resurrection is forever, never to die again
   - Likewise you also, RECKON YOURSELVES TO BE DEAD TO SIN, but ALIVE TO GOD
   - Therefore, DO NOT LET SIN REIGN IN YOUR MORTAL BODY
   - No longer instruments of unrighteousness to sin
   - Present yourselves to God as being ALIVE from the dead, and your members as instruments of RIGHTEOUSNESS to God
   - For sin shall NOT HAVE DOMINION OVER YOU…
   - For you are not under Law but UNDER GRACE

3) **DEPENDING ON THE POWER: The Holy Spirit… ...Romans 8:12**
   - "No condemnation to those who are in Christ Jesus"
   - "Who walk according to the SPIRIT"

- "The LAW OF THE SPIRIT OF LIFE in Christ Jesus"
- "MADE ME FREE FROM THE LAW OF SIN AND DEATH"

4) **RESULTS: VICTORY……………………Romans 8:11, 37**
   - The Holy Spirit of god dwells in the believer
   - The same Spirit that RAISED CHRIST FROM THE DEAD
   - This same Spirit of God will also give spiritual life to your mortal body
   - Yet in all these things we are MORE THAN CONQUERORS through Him (Christ) who loved us

LIVING A DEFEATED CHRISTIAN LIFE

1) **BY MY WORKS:** *(Galatians 2:16; Ephesians 2:4–10)*
- A man is not justified by the works of the Law
- A person is JUSTIFIED by FAITH in CHRIST JESUS

2) **BY TRUSTING IN MY PERFORMANCE** *(2 Corinthians 10:12; 2 Corinthians 5:12)*
- Comparing yourself to others is not wise
- They boast in appearance and not in heart

3) **DEPENDING ON SELF INSTEAD OF:** *(Hebrews 12:2; Proverbs 14:16; James 3:16)*
- LOOKING unto Jesus . . .A fool rages and is SELF-CONFIDENT Envy and SELF-SEEKING produce confusion and evil things

4) **RESULTS: Defeat** *(Leviticus 26:17; John 5:30; John 15:5)*
- I will set My Face against you and you SHALL BE DEFEATED by your enemies…
- I can of Myself do nothing…For without Me you can do nothing

ABUNDANT, VICTORIOUS LIVING

How to discern whether you are in the FLESH or in the SPIRIT
(Galatians 5:16–26)

Works of the Flesh	*Fruit of the Spirit*
Adultery, Fornication, Uncleanness, Lewdness, Idolatry, Sorcery, Hatred, Contentions, Jealousies, Outbursts of Wrath, Selfish Ambitions, Dissensions, Heresies, Envy, Murder, Drunkenness, Revelries	Love, Joy, Peace, Kindness, Longsuffering, Goodness, Faithfulness, Gentleness, Self-Control
"...Those who practice such things will NOT INHERIT the Kingdom of God."	"Against such there is no law. And those who are Christ's have CRUCIFIED the FLESH with its passions and desires."
The FLESH as an enemy is a New Testament idea, focusing the CARNAL, inbred tendencies of fallen humanity. When we allow the carnal mind to dominate our thinking, it will sooner or later result in activities that are flesh-oriented and at enmity with the SPIRIT.	"If we LIVE in the SPIRIT, let us also WALK in the SPIRIT." (v.26) Godliness and Moral Purity are the design of the Holy Spirit, as He develops in us "fruit" of the "Divine Nature." (II Peter 1:2–8)
LIBERTY (Galatians 5:1) – Can degenerate into License, but the Spirit enables us to subdue "the lust of the flesh" when we continuously submit ourselves to His Power and Control. "Walking in the Spirit" is an expression **which means LIVING one's life in the POWER of the SPIRIT** while being GUIDED by the Spirit.	The intended purpose is to constrain us toward a life in which the tendencies of the flesh are both undesirable and unproductive. Only the Holy Spirit in our spirit can produce this "fruit", and not our own efforts.

The works of the flesh are plural,
but the fruit of the Spirit is one and indivisible.

As stated in 2 Corinthians 5:17, if anyone is in Christ, he is a new creation. Spiritual things are always *new*—within the context of the Holy Spirit. The virtues listed in Galatians 5:22–23 are characterized as "fruit" in contrast to "works." Only the Holy Spirit can produce them, and not our own efforts.

In contrast to the fruit of the Spirit is "the lust of the flesh"—desire, or passion, from the Greek word *epithumia,* from the Greek work *thumos,* from which *thermos* and *thermostat* are derived. These ideas combine to indicate a "temperature" that may rise unbridled, calling for some means to regulate and direct passion toward proper and healthy, holy, spiritual application rather than carnal fulfillment.

Because the flesh desires to be:

Ratified—sanctioned or confirmed;

Gratified—pleasured or pleased;

Satisfied—satiated or filled full, maximized, believers must find the appropriate means of regulating and directing all our passions.

This text reveals that the Holy Spirit will: *(Galatians 5:16–23)*

1. Enable warfare against self-indulgent carnality (vv. 16–18).
2. Give discernment regarding what is unworthy (vv. 19–21)
3. Bring growth in character (vv. 22, 23)
4. Impart a readiness to live as dead to self but alive to Christ through His cross and resurrection

FEED YOUR FAITH AND YOU WILL STARVE YOUR FEARS

Feed on the Bread of Life Everyday

The disciples asked Jesus to "increase our faith." *(Matthew 17:20; Mark 11:22–24; Luke 17:5–6)* Jesus said, "If you have faith as a mustard seed, you can move mountains." *(Luke 8:11)* It's *not the size* of the seed; it's the *power* within the seed. The power in faith is *understanding how faith works.* That little seed will work and become a large tree.

Plant your faith in God. Start acting on that faith. Like a seed in the ground, it will take on the nature of a miracle in the making. Seeds that are planted, in time, will *break through* sidewalks, pavement, and any obstacle in their way.

ABOUT THE AUTHOR

Arnie Derksen was born and raised in northern Saskatchewan, Canada, to Mennonite parents. Being raised in church, Arnie's heart was toward the Lord, but after working with some charlatan evangelists and losing his mother to cancer, his faith was shaken. He then turned his full attention to the entertainment field and left the beliefs of his childhood. Arnie was successful as an entertainer in the Las Vegas and Florida nightclub circuits as well as entertaining on Canadian television and radio. He secured a recording contract with Decca Records and moved to Nashville, Tennessee. However, there was an emptiness within his life that money, fame, and success could not fill. It was then he began to search through eastern religions and Scientology for spiritual completeness.

Looking through the philosophy section of a bookstore in Flagstaff, Arizona, Arnie found a small book entitled *The Runner's Bible.* Intrigued when the author said to substitute the words "love" for God and "truth" for Jesus Christ, Arnie purchased the small volume and read it daily. Those were the things he had been searching for: love and truth. God saw the yearning in Arnie's heart for a true relationship with Him, and He intervened supernaturally as Arnie drove from Arizona to the Northwest. God stopped him on a highway in Mt. Lassen National Park, and Arnie got out of his car, kneeling by an old log, and received Jesus Christ as his personal Savior. The years of searching were over, and the life of knowing Jesus had begun.

Arnie attended Bible College and earned his Bachelor of Religious Education degree. His love for the Word of God permeated his life, and he began singing and speaking in churches across the United States and Canada. In 1976, he married Indy, and they began serving the Lord together through evangelistic work and pastoring.

This book began in the mid-'80s as a personal study. From time to time Arnie would revisit the manuscript, adding to it as the Lord inspired him. He began to share it with a few close friends, who encouraged him to publish the manuscript. When Arnie gave the rough draft to his pastor, Doctor Joshua Beckley of Ecclesia Christian Fellowship, he too urged Arnie to publish it in book form. Dr. Beckley even recommended a publishing company, headed by Lynn Williams. Lynn and her husband, Paul, always sat in the pew directly in front of the Derksens! What a wonderful God we serve! While this book was a long time coming, it has arrived to support the body of Christ in becoming authentic Christians.

CONTACT US:

We want to hear from you about this book. Also, if you are interested in a line of Christian books and want us to contact you on all new releases, please log on to: ***www.royalcandlelight.com*** *or* ***info@royalcandlelight.com***

Royal Candlelight Christian Publishing Company
"Royalty in the Making"

www.ingramcontent.com/pod-product-compliance
Lightning Source LLC
Chambersburg PA
CBHW060127050426
42448CB00010B/2029